COGNITIVE ADAPTATION

Cognitive Adaptation: A Pragmatist Perspective argues that there is a fundamental link between cognitive/neural systems and evolution that underlies
human activity. One important result is that the line between nature and
culture and scientific and humanistic inquiry is quite permeable – the two
are fairly continuous with each other. Two concepts figure importantly in our
human ascent: agency and animacy. The first is the recognition of another
person as having beliefs, desires, and a sense of experience. The second
term is the recognition of an object as alive, a piece of biology. Both reflect a
predilection in our cognitive architecture that is fundamental to an evolving,
but fragile, sense of humanity. The book further argues for a regulative norm
of self-corrective inquiry, an appreciation of the hypothetical nature of all
knowledge. Jay Schulkin's perspective is rooted in contemporary behavioral,
cognitive neuroscience and classical pragmatism.

Jay Schulkin is a research professor for the Departments of Physiology and
Biophysics and Neuroscience at Georgetown University. He is the author of
numerous texts, including *The Neuroendocrine Regulation of Behavior*, *Roots
of Social Sensibility and Neural Function*, *Bodily Sensibility: Intelligent Action*,
and *Allostasis, Homeostasis, and the Costs of Physiological Adaptation*.

Cognitive Adaptation

A PRAGMATIST PERSPECTIVE

Jay Schulkin

Georgetown University

CAMBRIDGE
UNIVERSITY PRESS

CAMBRIDGE UNIVERSITY PRESS
Cambridge, New York, Melbourne, Madrid, Cape Town, Singapore, São Paulo, Delhi

Cambridge University Press
32 Avenue of the Americas, New York, NY 10013-2473, USA

www.cambridge.org
Information on this title: www.cambridge.org/9780521517911

First published 2009

Printed in the United States of America

A catalog record for this publication is available from the British Library.

Library of Congress Cataloging in Publication Data

Schulkin, Jay.
    Cognitive adaptation : a pragmatist perspective / Jay Schulkin.
        p.   cm.
    Includes bibliographical references and index.
    ISBN 978-0-521-51791-1 (hardback)
    1. Cognition.   2. Adaptation (Physiology).   3. Neuropsychology.   I. Title.
    [DNLM: 1. Cognition.   2. Adaptation, Psychological.
    3. Psychophysiology. BF 311 S386c 2009]
    BF311.S3784   2009
    153–dc22   2008011617

ISBN   978-0-521-51791-1 hardback

For Jeffrey Rosen, Louis Schmidt, and David Weissman; I am very grateful for the love and support.

CONTENTS

PREFACE

This book emphasizes capturing the worth of human experience, the cognitive base of diverse forms of human activity, and the importance of dissolving the boundaries that decrease the pursuit of knowledge. The line between nature and culture and science and the humanities is and should be quite permeable, and the two are fairly continuous with each other. My hope is to demonstrate this permeability in my investigative approach.

The goal is a union of sorts through a regulative norm of self-corrective inquiry and an appreciation of the hypothetical nature of knowledge production and the embodied cognitive systems that reveal our diverse forms of interpretations and adaptation to circumstances.

Two concepts figure importantly with regard to human action: agency and animacy. The first is the recognition of another person as having beliefs, desires, a sense of experience. The second is the recognition of an object as alive, a piece of biology. Both reflect a predilection in our cognitive architecture and are fundamental to an evolving but fragile sense of humanity.

We need to be rooted to a sense of our evolution, our sense of living things. We need to develop sensibilities that highlight the importance of animate objects and recognize the beliefs and desires of others. Additionally, we need to further develop an educational sense rooted in history (a sense of agency), while still being mindful of the uncertain prospects and diverse threats.

My perspective is rooted in psychobiology, contemporary behavioral and cognitive neuroscience, and classical pragmatism.

I thank my friends, family, and colleagues for their help, as well as the two reviewers of this manuscript.

I miss very much my close friend and colleague John Sabini of the University of Pennsylvania, who died suddenly in August 2005, and with whom I spent years talking about most of the material in this book.

Introduction

Hope is the thing with feathers
That perches in the soul...
– Emily Dickinson

Ours is the age of biological knowledge. In the scope of its objectives and in its potential for transforming how we think about our place in the world, the Human Genome Project is the direct descendant of the Manhattan Project. This seemingly incongruous analogy has at its center the common theme of an assembly of scientists working together toward a common end and with great potential power. For the Human Genome Project, that end is deciphering the molecular composition of our genetic heritage.

Experiment lies at the heart of modern science (Dear, 1995; see also Bernard, 1865/1957). The idea of reconstructing who we are, of illuminating a moment in our evolutionary journey, and of knowing in full detail the underlying blueprint and structure of our biological material is the ultimate legacy of Charles Darwin and Gregor Mendel, arguably the progenitors of the modern biological sciences. The depiction of our entire genetic structure is as revolutionary as was Albert Einstein's reconstruction of the world of physics once inhabited by Isaac Newton.

We can only comprehend the radical nature of the Human Genome Project's import because we come prepared to understand the world in terms of agents and action, direction. We come prepared to share and exploit experiences, to form meaningful connections – to be connected to others (Jaspers, 1913/1997). In this introduction, I lay the groundwork for (1) an orientation toward understanding and creating living objects and (2) the behavioral/neural underpinnings of our understanding of the embodied states of others. The cognitive achievement of distinguishing animate from inanimate objects and then recognizing the beliefs and desires of others and their personal histories – a related but distinct cognitive adaptation – in part underlies both our evolution and the devolution of this function. Those facts, along with a general ability for self-corrective inquiry, underlie important cognitive achievements.

CREATING AND UNDERSTANDING LIVING THINGS. Imagine injecting a gene into a virus that is taken up by aberrant cells, thereby correcting for a genetic pathology. This scenario is no longer the stuff of science fiction but is fact. As they are perfected, gene therapy and similar methodologies will be used in the treatment of cystic fibrosis, cancers, hemophilia, and other ailments (see Figure I.1). Although never eradicated, our vulnerability to a variety of diseases and biological markers will be reduced and is being reduced to a molecular level of analysis (see Kitcher, 1996; Rosenberg, 2006).

Biological scientists can take great pride in these events while maintaining a sense that great events in science carry potential dangers. This is because science, as Sir Francis Bacon noted, is power. It can be used for noble, mundane, or atrocious purposes. Along with the great advances against human disease and suffering, both this century and the last bear testimony to science as a potentially devastating force.

Recall Mary Wollstonecraft Shelley's (1818/1976) great novel about the origins of Dr. Frankenstein's creation and the power of science. As we expand the biological sciences, fears of mimicking a creation like that of Frankenstein become omnipresent. Dr. Frankenstein's

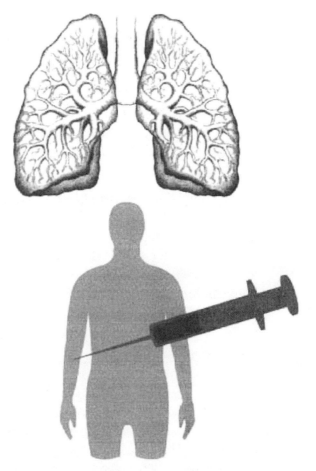

FIGURE I.1. A cartoon of injecting a gene that can correct for a disease of the lung like cystic fibrosis (Yansen & Schulkin, 2007).

nameless monster is a creature of our own making (see Figure I.2). We generated the power and knowledge to create this artificial man, yet the brute is a naive sort of blank slate on which the rest of humanity makes its imprint. He is not inherently evil, and he is without prejudice. Dr. Frankenstein yells out, "It's alive!" as he watches his creation move and gesture. But the consequences of the monster's agency, his aliveness, are dire.

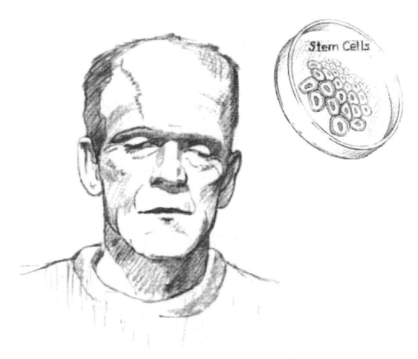

FIGURE 1.2. The monster of Dr. Frankenstein's creation (Yansen & Schulkin, 2007).

The world imposes, and the monster grows angry with disappointment and hurt. He begins to strike back and asserts to his creator:

> I am malicious because I am miserable. Am I not shunned and hated by all mankind? You, my creator, would tear me to pieces and triumph; remember that, and tell me why I should pity man more than he pities me? You would not call it murder if you could precipitate me into one of those ice-rifts and destroy my frame, the work of your own hands. Shall I respect man when he condemns me? Let him live with me in the interchange of kindness; and instead of injury I would bestow every benefit upon him with tears of gratitude at his acceptance. (Shelley 1817/1976, p. 130; see also McGinn, 1997/1999)

We have a cognitive capacity to distinguish the animate from the inanimate, but as our biological technologies surge forward, we begin to see a blurring of the conventional distinctions between the natural world and the cultural one that we have constructed. This is the world in which we are trying to create something alive. If science is humanized and directed by sanguine judgments, then perhaps the object lesson of Mary Shelley's *Frankenstein* appears less formidable.

The emphasis of the book is the sense of animacy coupled with our sense of agency. We are far from truly simulating such links between biological tissue and inorganic devices, but our ultimate goal is the fusion of the two, the creation of animate objects. The combination of the biological with the inanimate of our creation is something of our generation, for which Mary Shelley's premonition has furnished us with an orientation. The cognitive preconditions reflect our own predilection to understand the world in terms of the living and the nonliving, whether or not someone is an agent (with beliefs, desires, and experiences to be considered).

Creating our own tissue is a modern form of the fusion of our concept of animacy (i.e., something alive) with the new tools of information processing and molecular biology. We are only at the beginning of this fusion. We are not nearly close to talking about agency (Sabini & Schulkin, 1994; Sabini & Silver, 1982), but its roots rest in our cognitive predilection to distinguish the animate from the inanimate (see Carey, 1985/1987; Keil, 1983; Meltzoff, 2004).

We may, for example, ameliorate diverse kinds of learning disabilities through the use of stem cells. Stem cells are undifferentiated cells that may be useful in correcting cells that do not function well. It is conceivable that stem cell tissue can be used for a wide variety of neurological disorders that are important for cognitive systems that learn, remember, and are stable (Gage, 1998); it may enable the most debilitated among us to become functional members of society. This birth and rebirth is now close to being a scientific reality (e.g., Altman, 1966; Gould & McEwen, 1993; Kempermann, 2006; Ming & Song, 2005).

Rebirth and rejuvenation are at the heart of animate objects. In fact, it is possible that the fusion of our creation (stem cells) has the

potential to ameliorate diverse diseases, including autism – a state
in which one's sense of others' experiences is compromised (Baron-
Cohen, 1995/2000).

AUTISM AND THE UNDERSTANDING OF OTHER HUMAN BEINGS. We
are a species cognitively prepared to predict the behavior of others and
to understand others by the kinds of beliefs and desires that figure into
what they do, as well as what we predict they will do (e.g., Dennett,
1987; Premack, 1990). The devolution of this function is a feature
of decreased social competence (Baron-Cohen, 1995/2000; Schulkin,
2000, 2007b).

Agency and animacy are two cardinal features in our cognitive
lexicon that are replete with meaning, and that, in autistic individuals,
are impaired. The concept of agency, in the sense in which I use the
term, is tied to our beliefs, desires, preferences and goals, personal
histories, and historical legacies. Animacy is tied to agency, but it is not
the same; something can be alive without being an agent. The concept
is rooted in our intellectual history and originally tied to something
with a soul (or the Latin *anima*; Skrbina, 2005). Animacy is about
something being alive. There are diverse meanings of this term as it
applies to the concept of agency. The transition from something being
alive to something being an agent is (1) the instantiation of beliefs,
desires, and goals and (2) personal history (e.g., Dennett, 1987; Dewey,
1925/1989; Neville, 1974; Sterelny, 2000; Weissman, 2000).

These two categories of whether or not something is alive figure
importantly in our understanding of the world (Carey, 1985/1987; Keil,
1979, 2007) and are tied to our ability to determine diverse properties
of a thing. Our cognitive inclination is to explore when we have to,
when settled views are disrupted (Dewey, 1925/1989). This inclination
to explore and discover in the context of disrupted expectations is coupled with a keen sense for occasionally hitting on the right hypothesis
(Peirce, 1899/1992). Cognitive systems, in the sense I suggest, are nothing like the old Cartesian, divorced, distant arbiter. Rather, they are

about adaptation and action (see also Dewey, 1916; Lakoff & Johnson, 1999). Cognitive systems evolved to make sense of our surroundings and to problem solve; they are linked to engaged self-corrective inquiry (e.g., Anderson, 1997; Dewey, 1925/1989; Meltzoff, 2007).

There is an interface between simulated cognitive systems in diverse forms of material (e.g., chips) and biological material. There is also a confluence of the neural, psychological, and biological sciences in simulated forms of expression. Simulating diverse forms of biological functions, fusing the artificial with the biological, is part of the exciting age in which we live (Clark, 2003; Kitcher, 1996). Of course, we are more than the narrow notion of machines – those absolute clockwork devices envisioned in the seventeenth century (Descartes, 1644/1967). We are neither Cartesian machines thinking in a vacuum nor empirical blank slates (e.g., Levinson & Jaisson, 2006; Pinker, 2007). We bring with us diverse forms of cognitive devices that underlie the embodied experiences, what Dewey used to call "lived experiences," or what others have called "embodied cognition" (see Gallagher, 2005; Gibbs, 2006; Johnson, 2007; Lakoff & Johnson, 1999; Prinz, 2004; Schulkin, 2004; Varela, Thompson, & Rosch, 1991). Our cognitive evolution is reflected in the diverse expansion of these two categories across domains of biological and social interactions. Our devolution, a decrease in function, is also reflected in human pathology (Jackson, 1884/1958).

Decreased cognitive expression, such as toward agency and animacy, is a feature of autistic individuals. Autism involves social withdrawal, lack of eye contact, and lack of responsiveness to surrounding social situations (e.g., Baron-Cohen, 1995/2000). Recognizing the beliefs and desires of others is part of recognizing them as people who have experiences, who are agents (e.g., Fromm, 1947; Schulkin, 1992; Frith & Wolpert, 2003; Leslie, 1987). This sort of knowledge requires communication, making eye contact, touching one another, and forming meaningful bonds – something diminished by the cognitive competence of autistic individuals. These individuals may be good at solving mechanical problems, but they are severely limited in making social contact and at tasks that require focusing on another individual.

Two key cognitive features stand out in individuals with autism: they are more comfortable with less human contact and, in some instances (when controlling for IQ), are better able to solve problems that reflect mechanical (rather than personal) issues than are individuals without autism (Baron-Cohen, 1995/2000; Leslie, 1987). Although the ability to discriminate between animate and inanimate objects is present in autism, it is compromised (Baron-Cohen, 1995/2000). Autistic subjects often show a preference for inanimate objects and avoid human, animate contact. Autism is marked by a specific lack of interest in people and interpersonal interactions.

Shared human contact often entails looking into the eyes of another, watching what they are watching, and sharing experiences through vision (Baron-Cohen, 1995/2000; Tomasello, Carpenter, Call, Behne, & Moll, 2004). Experiments have consistently shown that autistic individuals have trouble sharing social contact through the visual system (Baron-Cohen, Tager-Flushberg, & Cohen, 1993/2000) – eye contact or gazing into the face of others is compromised (Baron-Cohen, 1995/2000; Specio et al., 2007). This is a fundamental impairment in gaining a foothold in the life world (Schutz, 1932/1967), the world of acknowledged human experiences, and in gaining fundamental human meaning through significant connections with others (Jaspers, 1913/1997).

Parsing out the social space of another human being, through the attribution of beliefs and desires, implies references to the experiences of others (e.g., Jaspers, 1913/1997; Mead, 1934/1972). After all, we believe that there is someone inside having an experience of one kind or another. Children fundamentally recognize animate objects very early on in ontogeny (Carey, 1985; Keil, 1987, 2007; Premack, 1990). Object contact, recognition of something as animate or inanimate (expressing intentional direction or not), is a fundamental cognitive tracking event of objects (Premack & Premack, 1983), and is one way in which we are rooted in our understanding of one another. Facial expressions, eye contact, and shared attention (e.g., shared mutual awareness of common focus) on someone's face are obviously important sources of information (Darwin, 1872/1965; Ekman, 1972). Young children and adults use this information in forming attachments. An appreciation of these events is compromised in autism (Baron-Cohen, 1995/2000, 2008; Dalton et al., 2005) and is more pronounced in boys generally (Baron-Cohen, Knickmeyer, & Belmonte, 2005).

Key neural structures underlie our sense of other people's beliefs and desires (e.g., Frith & Frith, 1999; Frith, 2007). For example, in brain-imaging studies under diverse experimental conditions, regions of the frontal cortex are activated when the person recognizes the experiences of others (e.g., Baron-Cohen 1995/2000). An early study using computerized photon emission tomography to measure blood flow as an index of neural activation showed increased activation of the frontal orbital field when subjects were asked to think about mental as opposed to physical words (e.g., Baron-Cohen, 1995/2000, 2008). The results suggested increased activation (greater blood flow) in the orbitofrontal cortex when subjects were attending to terms about beliefs and desires, as opposed to terms about bodily considerations.

The frontal cortex and other cortical sites, including the amygdala (old cortex), have since been shown to be significantly involved in recognizing the beliefs and desires of others (Frith & Frith, 1999). Using functional magnetic resonance imaging (fMRI), the brain regions that were activated in controls were the orbitofrontal cortex, superior temporal gyrus, and the amygdala (Baron-Cohen et al., 1999; Wang et al., 2004). Autistic subjects, on the other hand, showed compromised activation in both cortical sites and in the amygdala when compared to subjects who did not have autism (see Critchley et al., 2000; see also Amaral, Bauman, & Schumann, 2003; Ashwin, Baron-Cohen, Wheelwright, O'Riordan, & Bullmore, 2007; Frith & Frith, 1999).

Perhaps chemical signals in the brain (e.g., oxytocin) that are tied to attachment behaviors and that are compromised in autistic individuals (Carter, Lederhendler, & Kirkpatrick, 1997/1999; Insel & Fernald, 2004; Insel, O'Brien, & Leckman, 1999) could be ameliorated in part by stem cells that could turn into oxytocin cells in the brain. We know that autistic individuals have lower levels of oxytocin than age-matched controls (Modahl et al., 1998; Green, Fein, Modahl, Feinstein, Waterhouse & Morris, 2001) and can benefit somewhat from infusions of oxytocin and from treatments that affect oxytocin expression (Hollander et al., 2003; 2006), which serve to ameliorate some of the symptoms associated with autism (e.g., repetitive movements) that compromise behavioral adaptation. Importantly, an oxytocin receptor gene has been linked to autism (Wu et al., 2005), and oxytocin regulation in a number of species is fundamentally linked to diverse forms of attachment behaviors (Carter, 2007; Carter et al., 1997/1999; Lim, Bielsky, & Young, 2005) that are essential for getting a foothold in a world through contact with others.

Perhaps oxytocin levels could be rejuvenated in chemical composition by stem cells and thereby restore some of the human contact essential for normal development and successful adaptation through the restoration of neural function in diverse brain regions (e.g., amygdala, regions of the neocortex) (see Figure I.3).

Treatments for autism are an important scientific goal because the condition makes it difficult for people to function successfully, though they may have no physical problems and, in some cases, their intelligence is unimpaired. The pathology demonstrates the fundamental importance of agency and animacy to our interaction with the world.

COGNITIVE AND NEURAL PREDILECTION TO DETECT SELF-PROPEL-LED MOVEMENT. We are a species with elaborate taxonomic and thematic resources (e.g., Carey, 1985, 1987; Murphy, 2002). Understanding how the mind works entails understanding something about the

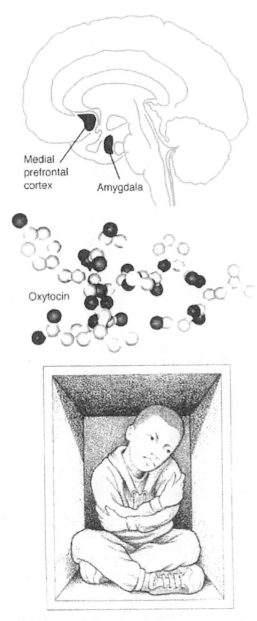

FIGURE I.3. Several regions of the brain knotted to social knowledge, oxytocin molecule, and an autistic child (adapted from Yansen & Schulkin, 2007).

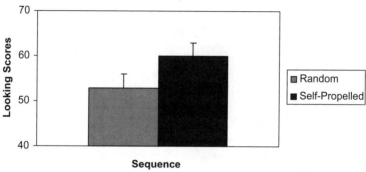

FIGURE I.4. Looking scores for the control (random) and experimental (self-propelled) sequences in preschool-aged children. Children looked longer at the experimental sequence after watching two previous control sequences than at the random sequence after two experimental habituation sequences (adapted from Dasser et al., 1989).

predisposition to invoke and impose some categories more than others (Hirschfield & Gelman, 1998).

Data suggests that the recognition of an object's motion is a primary perceptual event, rich in semantic possibilities. We come prepared to reason about the trajectory of objects (motion and trajectory of motivational states) and their being part of biological kinds (Leslie, 1987; Premack, 1990). What has not been resolved, particularly with regard to the central nervous system, is how specific the brain codes are for these categorical differences (e.g., Caramazza & Mahon, 2005; Caramazza & Shelton, 1998; Martin, 2007; Warrington & Shallice, 1984); perhaps the human nervous system is prepared to detect movement from animate objects and from inanimate objects (see Figure I.4) (Dasser, Ulbaek, & Premack, 1989; Premack, 1990).

The nervous system is oriented to recognize the detection of agency on the basis of features of movement. This is knotted to our ability to infer other people's self-propelled sense of movement (Premack, 1990). Different and overlapping regions of the brain may modulate

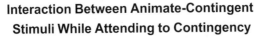

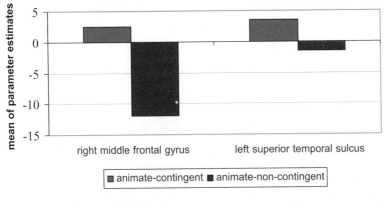

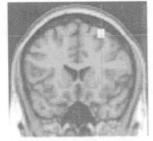

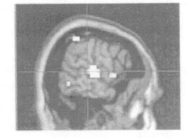

right middle frontal gyrus   left superior temporal sulcus

FIGURE I.5. Activation in the right middle frontal gyrus and left superior temporal sulcus occurs when participants are attending to the contingency (self-propelled condition) rather than detecting them on the basis of visual cues (adapted from Blakemore et al., 2003).

the perception of self-propelled action, as opposed to action forced on one. Diverse brain-imaging studies have shown that whether something is perceived as intentional and self-propelled is an important variable in activating a number of regions of the brain (e.g., right middle frontal gyrus, left superior temporal sulcus; see Blakemore et al., 2003; Castelli et al., 2000; Fogassi et al., 2005; Gallese, 2007) (see Figure I.5).

Interestingly, in experiments using fMRI, patterns of neural activity demarcated vignettes of social action from mechanical action (Martin & Weisberg, 2003; Weisberg, Turennout & Martin, 2006). The vignettes were not human or animal figures, only the configuration of shapes. Regions of the temporal lobe and amygdala linked to face recognition and more generally to animated or living objects (see also Martin, 2007; Martin, Ungerleider, & Haxby, 2000) were more active in the vignettes that depicted agency and social context than in the mechanically oriented vignettes (see Figure I.6).

In one of our most basic biological imperatives – the detection and interpretation of motion – we are already hardwired to look for agency and animacy.

INQUIRY, DOUBT, AND THE PRECARIOUS (A PRAGMATIST PERSPECTIVE). An embodied mind foraging for coherence, adapting to change, rich in sensorimotor function and corticalization of function, is important to the characterization of adaptive cognitive systems. And "every experience is a moving force" (Dewey, 1938/1972, p. 38) as we come prepared with an evolved brain and set of cognitive predilections that are situated toward context, flexibility, and perceptual embodiment about objects that are conceptually rich and vital to behavioral adaptation (e.g., Barsalou, 1999; Gibbs, 2006; Johnson & Rohrer, 2007; Shapiro, 2004).

Inquiry is an outgrowth of wanting to know. Self-corrective inquiry needs to be harnessed to the felt insecurity and uncertainty that are not just remnants of our biological past but endless lively events in our present context that are not likely to be eradicated. As John Dewey (1925/1989) would put it, we hunt for the stable amid the precarious (see also Godfrey-Smith, 1996, 2002).

Yet lurking within the mind/brain is unease about predators and concern about acquisition of food and shelter, along with unchecked levels of aspiration mixed with human gluttony. New identities

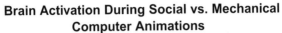

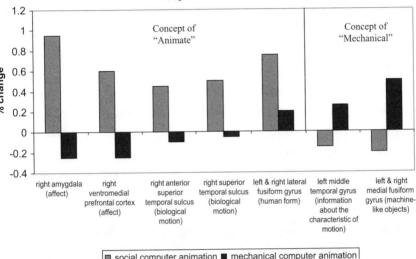

FIGURE 1.6. Concepts such as animate and mechanical may be generated from the interaction between "elemental processing capacities rather than as a manifestation of innately determined conceptual domains" (Martin & Weisberg, 2003, p. 584). For example, areas such as the amygdala, right ventromedial prefrontal cortex, right anterior superior temporal sulcus, right superior temporal sulcus, and left and right lateral fusiform gyrus, which are activated more during the social computer animations may represent the animate by processing information related to affect, biological motion, and human form. In contrast, areas such as left middle temporal gyrus and the left and right medial fusiform gyrus, which are activated during mechanical computer animations, may represent mechanical by processing information related to the characteristic of motion and machinelike objects (adapted from Martin & Weisberg, 2003).

are formed that, fashioned by diversity, generate novel expressions. Amusement and play are endemic to our condition to combat the insecurity and uncertainty of existence, but then so is our ability to eliminate thinking, to eschew it and forge into endless authorities.

We come into this world prepared to learn, inquire, and theorize. Whether or not this develops depends on the culture to which we are exposed, as well as the temperamental properties and abilities we possess. Self-corrective inquiry is the cornerstone of classical pragmatism (Smith, 1985) and is reflected in some variants of modern cognitive science (Gopnik et al., 2004; Meltzoff, 2007).

Cognitive systems are tied to our psychobiology, to the broad-based objects that we encounter, and to our brains (e.g., Gallistel, 1990; Lakoff & Johnson, 1999; Levinson, 1996, 2006). Cognitive systems reflect rough and ready heuristics that permeate problem solving (Gigerenzer & Selten, 2001; Simon, 1962), and not the Cartesian, almost-autistic mythology of perfection and detachment from seductive sensory pressures. We search for consistency and stability; we inquire and learn when our equilibrium is disrupted (Peirce, 1878; Rescorla & Wagner, 1972; Loewenstein, 1994), but not only under those conditions (Tolman, 1949).

To further explore that involved and off-kilter cognitive process, I have chosen just a subset of the questions about the human situation and have placed the philosophical issues they raise within the biological sciences. Chapter 1 discusses the contribution of cognitive systems to functional and adaptive representations. Chapter 2 considers how cognitive abilities function in the existential situations of life, of human evolution, when events are often beyond human control and make life uncertain and precarious. Chapter 3 advances beyond the "present" orientation of that discussion to elaborate on the distinction between memory, a cognitive trait humans share with many other animals, and a sense of history that defines cultural and human depth: the ultimate ends of human inquiry are to be understood in historical perspective. Chapter 4 discusses education and neurogenesis and emphasizes two points: the cultivation of vulnerability that reflects the fallibility of knowledge and the importance of actually engaging the issues of learning from one another's experiences. Chapter 5 focuses on religious inquiry, which arises from both cognitive predilections and the evolution of human beings in society. I suggest inquiry into the psychobiological sensibilities of natural piety. The concluding chapter addresses several themes of embodied cognition, demythologized reason, and cognitive adaptation amid a larger vision of self-corrective inquiry that can serve human flourishing.

1

Cognitive Adaptation, Objects, and Inquiry

It is impossible to know intuitively that a given cognition is not determined by a previous one.
– C. S. Peirce, *Questions Concerning Certain Faculties Claimed by Man*, 1868

Psychobiological propensities stem from the constraints of the human mind/brain and its computational abilities. We are born with diverse forms of cognitive abilities; there should be no mythology about this. The question is, "To what degree?" and here there are legitimate disputes. Our hypothesis-generating abilities exist in the specific culture in which we are immersed, and that shapes our thinking (Mill, 1843/1873; Peirce, 1899/1992); however, some of the categories reflect the cognitive machinations of the mind/brain and how it operates in problem solving with nature and other sentient creatures.

Common categories into which we can organize our responses are those that we inherit and those that we acquire (e.g., Carey & Smith, 1993; Gelman, 2003; Levinson, 1996, 2006; Medin & Atran, 1999). The process of evolution selected for a self-corrective capacity in our ability to get anchored to the world around us (Darwin, 1859/1958; Dewey, 1910/1965). Dewey, for example, understood that science, in part, is an extension of local adaptation or local problem solving.

This chapter focuses on the logic of inquiry from a pragmatist perspective, which, along with a cognitive and/or functional predilection toward kinds of objects, underlies the organization of action (see Johnson, 2007; Schulkin, 2004). Cognition functions in the context of adaptation and action. Cognitive systems are endemic to the organization of action, a common theme for pragmatists (e.g., Dewey, 1896). Two key categories are essential: a recognition of the kinds of objects in terms of animate and inanimate objects and a sense of agency or lived experience (Dewey, 1925/1989).

CORE PROBLEM SOLVING. Inquiry takes place in the life world of agents and animate objects (e.g., Heelan, 1983; Kuhn, 2000; Schutz, 1932/1967). Concepts such as agency and animacy are background categories that underlie our inferences, our understanding of the objects around us. We infer or deduce or induce events against this background framework.

Abduction is a term that C. S. Peirce (1878, 1899/1992) coined for hypothesis formation: the genesis of a theory or idea that in turn guides the inference of conclusions, whether by induction or deduction (see also Dewey, 1938; Hanson, 1958/1972; Heelan & Schulkin, 1998). By providing the background against which observations are made (in addition to participating in a culture of inquiry), abduction links ideas to reality, as well as to deduction and induction functions in human problem solving. Peirce's concept generates cognitive models of human information processing and reasoning that underlie decision making and human action (Johnson-Laird, 2002; Levi, 2004).

The range of possible hypotheses is constrained by abduction, where seeing an object as something already presupposes some context of understanding (e.g., Hanson, 1958/1972; Lakoff & Johnson, 1999; Sellars, 1962, 1968; Wittgenstein, 1953/1968) in which highlighting central tendencies about object relationships, for instance, and inductive inferences are placed in a warranted context (Barsalou, 2003; Gopnik et al., 2004; Levinson, 2006; Medin & Atran, 2004). Thus the inductive mechanisms are not random, and the deductive mechanisms not so distant, because they are knotted to abduction. Our inferences are constrained by an orientation to events, the kinds of objects that we detect. Linking together animals, say, mammals, as animals that bear live young, and finding what seem like counterexamples (e.g., the platypus, an egg-laying mammal), first requires a broad way to link diverse kinds of events, which may (perceptually) or may not (conceptually) have clear common properties (Mandler, 2004; Prinz & Barsalou, 2000). The taxonomic and thematic conditions may be simple or complex, but there is always some background condition (e.g., Giere, 2006; Medin & Atran, 1999, 2004; Murphy, 2002). Moreover, inductive devices are broadly conceived in a mind/brain ready to compute statistical probability, to draw diverse inferences, and to construct models (Johnson-Laird, 2001) essential for information processing and coherent action. These cognitive events are apparent in the taxonomic organization of basic objects (e.g., plants, animals) in diverse human societies (Aristotle, *De Anima*; Atran et al., 1999; Atran, Medin, & Ross, 2005).

COGNITIVE PRECONDITIONS, OR MAKING SENSE OF LIVING THINGS: RELATIONS BETWEEN BIOLOGY AND CULTURE. Key categories about kinds of objects pervade the epistemological landscape. Cognitive predilection underlies action and inquiry (e.g., Dewey, 1896; Gallistel, 1990; Lakoff & Johnson, 1999). Categories of understanding converge at every step in our intellectual development (Cassirer, 1944/1978, 1953/1957), and symbolic and computational systems permeate all levels of human understanding. Generic categories, of kinds both naturally and culturally derived, are operative early on in ontogeny (Carey & Gelman, 1991; Gelman, 2003; Keil, 1979, 1983). An orientation toward biological events may be a core disposition in our cephalic organization (e.g., Keil, 1979, 2007; Waxman, 2007).

Table 1.1 depicts one set of relationships that reflects an orientation toward taxonomic categories of living things.

In other words, we are prepared to generate a range of categories quite early – animate and inanimate, animal and plant, objects in space, and so on (see Carey, 1985/1987, 2001; Deheane, Izard, Pica, &

TABLE 1.1.

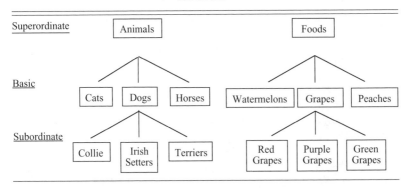

Source: Waxman, 1999.

Spelke, 2006; Duchaine, Cosmides, & Tooby, 2001; Keil, 1987; Mandler, 2004; Pinker, 2007). We are taxonomic animals; we categorize things (Carey & Gelman, 1991; Keil & Wilson, 2000; Levinson, 2003), and we come prepared to discern events from a core orientation and perspective (e.g., the solidity of objects; Saxe, Tzelnic, & Carey, 2006; Spelke, Phillips, & Woodward, 1995). Both Boston natives and Amazonian indigenes use points, line parallel construction, and angles to discern distal nonobvious objects; they are cognitive adaptations in basic object understanding (Deheane et al., 2006).

We readily accept certain categories and look for certain objects in our surroundings (Barkow, Cosmides, & Tooby, 1992; Carey & Gelman, 1991; Medin & Atran, 1999). Environmental factors are essential in understanding our cognitive capabilities (Clark, 1999; Gibson, 1966), and a preparedness to note diverse relationships may reflect a form of folk biological discourse (e.g., avoiding foul meat, searching for warmth and security, connecting with others in common bonds, expressing ourselves in symbolism rich in cognitive prowess).

A study of the Mayan lowlands of Guatemala shows how kinds of objects are understood relative to an orientation, for example, a characterization expressing how diverse groups understand nature (Atran et al., 1999). The Mayan lowlands is an area rich with diverse

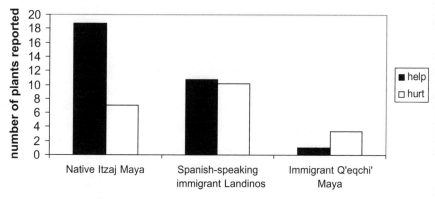

FIGURE 1.1. The number of plants reported for three different groups and their relationship in terms of whether they were helped or hurt by people-plant interactions. *Source:* Adapted from Atran et al. (1999).

cultures. Three basic groups coincide: indigenous Itzaj Maya, immigrant Q'eqchi' Maya, and Spanish-speaking individuals of mixed European/Amerindian descent (Landinos) (Atran et al., 1999). They all live in the same habitat, yet they all have different views and different responses to the care of nature. All three cultural groups work from a different theory of the objects in their natural environment. Diverse taxonomic characterization is the staple of cognitive coherence. But there is wide variation and diversity in our cognitive machinations and what we emphasize and what we do not. Some groups may even show devolution of function about natural objects (Wolff & Medin, 2001; Atran & Medin, 2008).

For instance, in the Guatemalan study, the native Maya do the most to help sustain the surrounding environment (Atran et al., 1999, 2005; Medin & Atran, 2004) (see Figure 1.1). The native Maya also possess more expertise about natural objects in their terrain, not surprisingly, than do the other two groups. Nevertheless, each has diverse cognitive categories for understanding plants and animals. But the concept of an animate object is a basic one that they all share.

CHILDREN'S ANIMATE/INANIMATE DISTINCTIONS. Children's cognitive abilities are reflected in their representations and expression of symbolism (Piaget, 1954). Children are neither "blank slates," nor inherently riddled with a "blooming buzzing confusion" as James (1890/1917) theorized. Research in developmental psychology has expanded on the work of Piaget, suggesting that children impose order early on, much earlier than Piaget postulated (see Carey, 1985/1987; Mandler, 2004).

Children track objects; generate inferences to background orientations that provide perspective; and use time, probability of events, familiar-unfamiliar comparisons, and other cognitive devices early on in ontogeny. Even very young infants are quite capable, for example, of determining something about object direction and object motion (Spelke et al., 1995; Gelman & Markman, 1987). Children's orientation to others reflects their fundamental recognition of animate self-propelled objects (Carey, 1985/1987).

Piaget (1954, 1972) argued that young children are animistic (on the concept as applied to primitive thinking, see also Durkheim, 1915/1965; Frazer, 1922/2000; Malinowski, 1948). He stated that they overattribute the concept of animacy to more objects than they should. But the concept of animism is a fundamental category in our lexicon, playing diverse roles in the organization of action (e.g., Bird-David, 1999; Premack, 1990).

Research has shown that children are not as animistic as had been originally thought. Within the first few years, children distinguish animate from inanimate objects (Carey, 1985/1987; Gelman, Spelke, & Meck, 1983; Keil, 1979). One study by Dolgin and Behrend (1984) found that animism is not an all-pervasive phenomenon in young children, not an unconstrained cognitive attribution. Young children rarely made mistakes distinguishing between prototypical animate

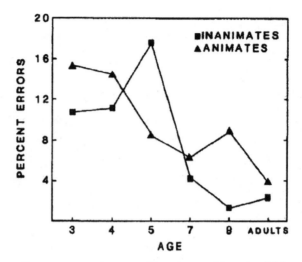

FIGURE 1.2. Response to animate and inanimate objects in children. *Source:* Dolgin and Behrend (1984).

and inanimate objects. They are not necessarily prone to overattribute the concept of animacy to inappropriate objects. Interestingly, children who were tested with less prototypical objects were more likely to make errors. Human beings may be overprepared to attribute the concept of animacy and to infuse objects with rich symbolic expression, but they quickly learn to limit the attribution (see Figure 1.2).

The ability to demonstrate knowledge of the boundary conditions of animate objects is first expressed early and is not necessarily indiscriminate. Humans use the concept less indiscriminately than Piaget seems to have believed. This is a fact about our cognitive capabilities, and not a trivial one (Gelman et al., 1983). Importantly, looking to detect self-propelled objects (Mandler, 2004; Premack, 1990) and linking this understanding to internal causation is one anchor in the detection of animate versus inanimate objects (Leslie, 1987; Wellman, 1990).

The attribution of a category, such as agency or animacy, is not all or none, and it expands as greater accuracy and the expression of knowledge deepen theorizing (Gelman, 2003). Category attribution is oriented toward starting with things that move and that are self-generated (Mandler, 2004; Premack, 1990). Aristotle recognized this human penchant in *De Anima*, describing the notion of kinds and causal efficacy (Lennox, 2001). Along with categorization, inductive mechanisms start early and are grounded in diverse forms of orientation to events (e.g., Medin & Atran, 2004). Induction is couched in an orientation; abductive mechanisms (the tendency to hit on the right idea; e.g., bats being mammals) are used because young children are grounded in both taxonomic and deductive mechanisms and naturally seek consistency.

Young children also recognize that natural events can occur independently of human action (e.g., Gelman, Durgin, & Kaufman, 1995). Moreover, children believe that animals and inanimate objects are expressions of different kinds of motion or movement. In fact, children may appreciate that an animal or thing can cause its own movement before understanding how that can occur; the storehouse of knowledge grows amid a basic framework.

With regard to children's understanding of animacy and agency, it is much debated how early and how deep the orientation is. We do know, again, that the concept of animacy is not as pervasive (i.e., unrestrained) in young children's thinking as Piaget suggested. However, Piaget was right to highlight the importance of animacy in understanding the world around us; there is substantial evidence that children are equipped with such orientations early in life, and that the animate-inanimate categorization is one of them.

Neonates look to determine changes, abrupt or not (Gopnik et al., 2004; Kagan, 1984, 2002). They encounter objects that appear and disappear and are coded relative to a background set of cognitive assumptions – all of which are not accessible to the contents of consciousness. In fact, very little of the cognitive arsenal is accessible to consciousness (Rozin, 1976, 1998). The child is aware, conscious, before the onset of language, but language changes everything in the diverse cognitive systems that are at work.

Thus, William James (1890/1917; 1910/1970) mistakenly, as I have indicated, said that the child's world at first is "a blooming, buzzing confusion" upon which, over time, the culture imposes concepts that provide order. This view suggests that, as a child accommodates externally imposed events, his or her ability to use concrete, stimulus- or sign-driven representations develops into the ability to use symbolic representations. This was also the view of Piaget, who claimed that children are simply concrete in their perceptions and abilities at birth and develop abstract abilities with the acquisition of concepts. Although this notion is at least partly true, more recently it has been shown that children can also conceptualize space, time, and probability, and that they order their worlds from the beginning (Carey, 1983; Spelke et al., 1995).

Implicit in Piaget's (1954, 1971/1975) assimilation-accommodation theory is the idea of conceptual growth in response to new stimuli that occur within a context of interest to the child. But children do not begin with incoherence and forge coherence as they develop (Kagan, 1984). Rather, they begin with concepts and computations about objects in space (e.g., Carey, 2001; Carey & Gelman, 1991; Deheane et al., 2006; Spelke et al., 1995) that are influenced by diverse background frames of reference (Alloway, Corley, & Ramscar, 2006; Levinson, 2003, 2006).

Young children look to impose conceptual coherence, and they search for stable, essential features that inhere in objects (Gelman, 2003). Humans create organization around diverse kinds of entities and readily distinguish essential and conditional features of objects – particularly the fundamental animate-inanimate distinction and its rich symbolic expression in the objects that give meaning to our lives.

OBJECT-ORIENTED COGNITIVE SYSTEMS. Amid the development of perceptual competence, cognitive events occur, rich in information processing. These include the creation of conceptual categories (Keil, 1979; Keil & Wilson, 2000; Mandler, 2004) and the imposition of diverse categories against background theory (Hanson, 1958/1972; Lakoff & Johnson, 1999; Medin & Atran, 2004; Murphy, 2002). Such cognitive events, whether implicit or explicit, provide coherence and underlie the organization of action. They are used to pick out kinds of objects and to track events.

Keeping track of objects (Sterelny, 2003) and looking to determine essential features (if there are any), both apparent and not, are fundamental cognitive events (e.g., Kripke, 1980; Quine, 1969; Weissman, 2000) and figure importantly in the development and expression of thought (Gelman, 2003). Young children fix reference to objects, even though the original features may not determine how that object is understood. An orientation to core features, essential features that may or may not be manifest, is an organizing principle. The rich extension of concepts, such as animacy and agency, is expanded and extended to many objects in our world.

COGNITIVE ADAPTATION, BODILY SENSIBILITY, AND OBJECTS. The sense of objects is rooted in bodily sensibility (Johnson, 1987/1990, 2007; Lakoff & Johnson, 1999; Merleau-Ponty, 1942/1967). Objects are not detached; knowledge is accumulated via transactions with others (Clark, 1999; Dewey, 1925/1989; Mead, 1934/1972; Schulkin, 2004; Thomas, 2001; Varela, Thompson, & Rosch, 1991). Our cognitive functional adaptations reflect diverse forms of bodily sensibility (e.g., Barsalou, 2003) that are captured across anatomical networks in the brain (Martin, 2007). Sensorimotor features reflect a deep part of our cognitive capabilities (e.g., Dewey, 1925/1989; Lakoff & Johnson, 1999). Cognitive systems are endemic to the organization of perception, and perception is at the heart of action (e.g., Prinz & Barsalou, 2000).

The concept of embodiment has several meanings (e.g., Gibbs, 2006; Johnson & Rohrer, 2007; Rohrer, 2001; Wilson, 2002), but the one that I have in mind is the non-Cartesian account: representations of objects, such as whether something is animate or inanimate, are not isolated but endemic to the organization of action and human experience. Representations do not cut us off from the world of objects; indeed, cognitive systems are vehicles for engagement with others (Dewey, 1925/1989; Mead, 1934/1972; Schulkin, 2004). This is particularly apparent with regard to the consideration of agency and human action.

Lakoff and Johnson (1999), among other investigators (e.g., Barsalou, 2003; Gibbs, 2006; Wilson, 2002), have suggested that cognitive systems are rooted in action (Dewey, 1925/1989; Schulkin, 2007a). Cognitive adaptation is understood as in part (adapted from Lakoff & Johnson, 1999):

1. Thinking is perceiving.
2. Knowing is seeing.
3. Representing as doing.
4. Communicating as showing.
5. Searching as knowing.
6. Imagining as moving.
7. Attempting to gain knowledge is searching.
8. Becoming aware is noticing.
9. Knowing from a perspective is seeing from a point of view.

Thinking, that is, has to be understood in the context of action, of transacting with others, and is quite close to a pragmatist position, in which cognitive systems are embedded in the organization of action (see also Dewey, 1910/1965; James, 1890, 1917; Johnson, 1987/1990, 2007; Schulkin, 2004). The emphasis is on embodied cognitive systems (Barsalou, 2003; Wilson, 2002), and the sensorimotor systems are themselves knotted to cephalic machinations across all regions of the brain (see also, e.g., Barton, 2004, 2006; Dewey, 1896, 1938; Schulkin, 1992, 2007a). In other words, cognitive systems are not just a cortical affair; they are endemic to cephalic function.

COGNITIVE FEATURES IN NATURE AND CULTURE. Distinctions between concepts in nature and culture blur as inquiry progresses (Clark,

1999; Dewey, 1925/1989). Concepts of nature have their roots in biology, and concepts of culture derive from our cognitive capacity. We are as condemned by, or embedded in, one as we are the other. The study of culture is the study of variation amid some common themes (e.g., Atran et al., 2005; Boyd & Richerson, 1985; Mead, 1928, 1964).

Concepts of culture and nature are therefore intertwined. It is not simply from within culture that we evolved our categories and concepts. Categories of space, time, causation, the structure of syntax, and so forth, are conditions of the human mind that set the stage for the development of a culture (Atran, 2002; Cassirer, 1944/1978; Pinker, 1994, 1997; Reschler, 2000; Sperber, 1975, 1985). This is the functionalist position, which envisions the mind as adaptive and problem solving (Clark, 1999; Parrott & Schulkin, 1993).

Such problem solving, extended into social bonding – ways of conceiving social relationships, recognition of facial and bodily gestures – serves to guide us in the world. And anthropological inquiry reveals the myriad cognitive systems that are operative in the human condition (e.g., Boyer, 1990). Our cognitive abilities are both specific and general (Rozin, 1976, 1998). Cognitive flexibility is a central feature of our problem solving proclivities (Mithen, 1996).

An evolutionary perspective suggests, with regard to human problem solving, a greater expression, extension, and access of core adaptations (Rozin, 1976, 1998), and of use of cognitive resources in expanding domains of human interactions (Carey & Gelman, 1991; Mithen, 1996). In other words, core features that go into self-corrective inquiry include an orientation toward the observation of objects, the abduction or the genesis of ideas, the tying of ideas about the world to causation, and the development of diverse tools that expand one's observations (e.g., Gigerenzer, 2000; Hanson, 1958/1972; Heelan & Schulkin, 1998; Peirce, 1892; Sellars, 1962).

That humans construct worlds of perception; however, experience does not mean that there is no "real" world (e.g., Peirce, 1899/1992; Weissman, 2008). Within a biological context, problem solving is always adaptive. If an animal cannot see an object, it compensates with another sense, such as hearing or smell. The lenses from which we interpret the world are all theory laden; nothing is given (e.g., Hanson, 1958/1972; Heelan & Schulkin, 1998; Medin & Atran, 2004). Inferences take place within an orientation to events, and our orientations toward objects are part of the adaptive specializations of animals that create a world for action. It is intelligent action that we witness in the natural world (Hauser, 2000; Marler, 1961; Pinker, 1997, 2007; Smith, 1977).

Conceptualizations of nature have a rich history, both from a cultural standpoint and in that we are prepared to understand nature. Basic categories that set the conditions for understanding pervade our reasoning. Such basic core conceptions reflect the development of a cognitive apparatus under the pressure of natural selection.

Perhaps one should accept that there are psychobiological and genetic constraints on what, when, and how much humans can learn (e.g., Levinson & Jaisson, 2006; Marler, 2000; Pinker, 1994). Evolution does not hang on one cognitive feature, but on diverse kinds of cognitive abilities (see Rozin, 1976, 1998). We passed through phases in our cultural evolution from mythmaking to theorizing, problem solving, and testing (Dewey, 1916, 1938). Cognitive abilities are part of communicative competence, which is the mainstream of survival and the evolution and expression of intelligence, but mythmaking (storytelling and communicating with others through those tales) figures importantly. Responding to diverse forms of complexity reflects our cognitive architecture and our evolution (e.g., Dewey, 1925/1989; Godrey-Smith, 1996; Rozin, 1976; Sterelny, 2003).

Diverse kinds of cognitive systems, as I have indicated, reflect adaptive systems that connect us to the world – not something that separates us from events to which we are trying to adapt (Anderson, 1990; Gallistel, 1990; Jackendoff, 1992; Prinz & Barsalou, 2000). Our cognitive resources are tied to the fact that we are inherently social and tied to others (Levinson & Jaisson, 2006; Mead, 1932/1980, 1934/1972). The social milieu and transactions among us reflect the cephalic machinations of our species (Barton, 2004, 2006; Dunbar, 1992, 2003); an "interactive engine" is what pervades the social milieu (Levinson, 2006), with specific systems for understanding animate agents (Wheatley, Milleville, & Martin, 2007). Some of the brain regions linked to our social competence are depicted in Figure 1.3 (Adolphs, 1999; Adolphs & Spezio, 2006).

SYMBOLIC MEANINGS. With the emergence of symbolic representations came an evolutionary leap in our conceptual abilities (Donald, 2004), and diverse cognitive abilities constitute what it takes to be symbolic (e.g., Atran et al., 2005; Deacon, 1997; Sperber, 1985).

Cognitive competence pervades the use of symbols (Sperber, 1975, 1985). The nature of our symbols is reflected in the structure of myths (Levi-Strauss, 1962/1966), our psychology (Freud, 1924/1960), and the nuances of language (Dewey, 1938/1972; Levinson, 2006; Pinker, 2006; Sperber, 1975, 1985).

Cognitive prowess enables humans to prevail over nature, but other animals respond to events typically, presupposing the existence of certain conditions (e.g., time, space, gravity, edible objects) that organize human behavioral responses (Rozin, 1976; Gallistel, 1990; Marler, 2000). Symbolic expression permeates our understanding and extension of the concepts of animacy and agency as we extend them to new objects.

Concepts of animacy are infused with symbolic meaning, and when that happens, there can be no part of the brain that is involved with thought that is not also infused with symbolic meaning. The ability to use symbols is an adaptation, an evolutionary success story. In manipulating symbols, human beings harness the objects of the environment into a conceptual framework that gives them meaning. Symbolic representation probably emerged from a rudimentary stage in which early humans represented the objects they used and encountered to comprehend them. Cassirer (1944/1978, p. 24) posits that the use of symbols is "the distinctive mark of human life" that provides

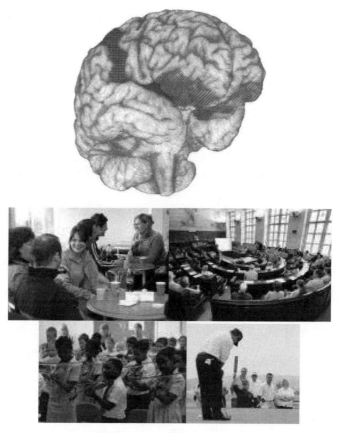

FIGURE 1.3. Some of the neuroanatomical structures involved in social cognition. *Note:* Diagonal lines are within the ventromedial prefrontal cortex, black area is within the insula cortex, dotted area is the amygdala, crosshatching is within the somatosensory cortex (courtesy of Ralph Adolphs).

a "new dimension of reality" (Cassirer, 1946; Langer, 1937; Sperber, 1975). Symbols themselves are forms of knowledge that communities share (Levi-Strauss, 1962/1966; Sperber, 1975). Thus, symbolic thought is pervasive in human reasoning and rooted in culture (Humbolt, 1836/1971; Levi-Strauss, 1962/1966).

Even if one were to presume a symbolic function in animals, human beings have a much greater facility for symbolic creation, use, and response than does any other species of animal. In the bio-logical and cultural evolution of humanity, there was a stage when our distant ancestors crossed a threshold from the presymbolic to the symbolic (Mithen, 1996, 2006) (see Figure 1.4). Underlying this shift were diverse cognitive adaptations that included knowledge of objects, social knowledge, and expansion of our problem solving and technical capabilities (Mithen, 1996, 2006).

It is a speculative venture to investigate the origins of humans' symbol use (Mithen, 1996, 2006), but speculation can surely take us down some interesting paths. We, nonetheless, are reminded of the cave paintings in Europe and the rock paintings of North America and Africa. All these depictions tend to repeat images, which suggests a broad agreement in the use and meaning of certain symbols. What do these images imply? Those who have studied cave and rock art have come up with many interpretations, but the drawings seem to have expressed the desire to represent what is familiar, and more important, to capture something about its meaning. There does seem to be a deep desire to "own" something, to become closer to it by representing it. After all, humans are epistemological animals; we want to understand our world, and so depict it. Perhaps it is just like giving something a name – visual naming. For example, in a number of religions, naming objects corresponds with divining them.

During ephemeral moments of safety, humans reflected. We began to consider the world and come to terms with it. We started to rep-resent what we saw. Early cave paintings and rock art provide an outlook on that seminal world (see Figure 1.5). These were not sophis-ticated conceptualizations; those were to come later, with the evolved perspectives of a seasoned mind and improved tools. Interestingly, young children and autistic individuals often depict animals in sim-ilar dimensions to early art. Perhaps they represent similar attempts to reflect and depict the world (Humphrey, 2000; Guthrie, 2005). These are adaptive responses to attempt to tame the perplexities of uncertainty and insecurity. Human understanding lies in the ability

Cognitive Adaptation

Social, technical and natural history intelligence
Art, religion and science.

Natural history and technical intelligence
Specialized technology. Animals and plants as "artifacts."

Social and natural history intelligence
Anthropomorphism (animals and plants as people). Totemism (people as animals).

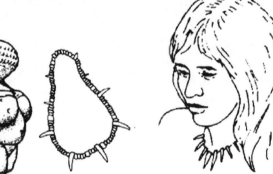

Social intelligence

Natural history intelligence

Technical intelligence

Language

General intelligence

Social and technical intelligence
People as "artifacts."
Artifacts for social interaction.

FIGURE 1.4. A depiction of cognitive evolution. *Source:* Mithen (1996).

to secure stability and security in representing events (Dewey, 1925/ 1989).

European cave paintings are often found deep within the caverns, a fact that has been much discussed. A trip into the dark recesses of a cave surely would not have been made casually. That so many of the visual representations are found there may indicate the importance

FIGURE 1.5. Cave painting.

placed on the process of painting the cave wall, and of the pictures themselves. Even the darkness may have had its own symbolic quality at that stage of humankind, much as it still does. It could have been a representation of the unknown and dangerous, overshadowed by a desire to bring it to light in the form of understanding and safety.

We might imagine the response of our ancestors to unexpected darkness, such as that of a solar eclipse. For some creatures, an eclipse may be a nonevent because they remain oblivious to a break in the normal cycle of dark and light. Birds, for instance, respond to an eclipse by going through their normal evening rituals, but it does not appear to alarm or frighten them. Perhaps at some stage in human evolution, humanity, too, was oblivious to an eclipse as anything special. Creatures with a more integrated and symbolized notion of the world – a day that is measured, a sun that is round and yellow, darkness that comes gradually – might be disturbed by an eclipse and, as with the darkness of the cave, need to have a sense of control over it. For example, animals that represented threats, food, companionship, and perhaps the inexplicable, became symbolic elements repeated throughout the caves and rock cliffs of our earliest art. Now that the representational function of painting has been replaced by photography, modern art may still express the rawest of those emotions.

CONCLUSION. The brain is designed for problem solving (e.g. Gazzaniga, 1995/2000; James, 1890/1917). Cognition systems traverse the whole of the nervous system and underlie all human activity (Barton, 2004, 2006; Schulkin, 2007a). A toolbox of prepared cognitive systems is part of the arsenal of adaptation to our surroundings, one of which is the concept of living things (Carey, 1985/1987; Medin & Atran, 2004).

Diverse forms of taxonomic and thematic orientations set the foundations for human problem-solving proclivities, which have been expanded and extended in expression (Rozin, 1976, 1998). Human symbolic representations are an extension of us, of what we are coping with, of what we are trying to understand or conquer and become at peace with in everyday adaptations (Clark, 1999; Levinson, 2006). Symbols line our world and infuse our very sense of objects; that is, any object of the natural world is infused with symbols. Symbols inhere in the life worlds that pervade our experiences.

Core concepts, such as animacy and agency (the detection of the beliefs and desires of others, and their embodiment in individuals), in addition to senses of space, time, probability, and language, figure in the rich symbols that permeate our world (e.g., Kitcher, 1990; Pinker, 1994, 1997). These cognitive abilities are intertwined and reflect everyday activities. Diverse kinds of cognitive systems set the conditions for how to respond to the uncertainty, the conditions for historical cohesion, for educational embrace, and for meaningful adventures, all of which should be harnessed to self-corrective inquiry.

The cognitive, in addition to cultural milieu, sets the context for human expression. Our minds and the tools we invent coevolve, reflecting our biological legacy (Barton, 2004, 2006; Mellars, 1996, 2006). Both demonstrate the ways we humans have learned to cope with our surroundings and forge social links with one another (e.g., Clark, 2003). Social intelligence is a primary feature in human evolution (e.g., Dunbar, 1992, 1996; Humphrey, 1976). That intelligence is made possible by language and diverse forms of cognitive abilities.

2

The Human Situation:
Uncertainty and Adaptation

When students of mental evolution discovered how great a role
symbols have played in science, they were not slow to exploit that
valuable insight.
    – Susanne Langer, *Philosophy in a New Key*

Humans in the modern world still dwell in a world of contingency and
abject uncertainty. Amid this uncertainty is the use of instrumental
reason – reason devoted to coping with the lack of certainty in the
search for the stable and somewhat secure. Although this state may
create great grief and angst (e.g., Heidegger, 1927/1962), it also prompts
action and inquiry. Pragmatists such as Dewey emphasized the plasticity of the modern world, the many diverse forms of adaptation and
human expression (Margolis, 2002). Dewey (1925/1989) also noted,
perhaps somewhat hopefully, that "the natural and original bias of
man is all toward the life objective" (p. 14).

    Problem solving is rooted in the existential condition of coping
with our surroundings. Knowing occurs in interactions with others
and with the world, which is a core pragmatist perspective. The knowing process takes place in the life world that we are adapting to, coping
with, and trying to make sense of (Dewey, 1925/1989; Godfrey-Smith,
2002).

    This chapter begins with an evolutionary account of the cogni-
tive/behavioral adaptations that underlie our sense of agency and
inquiry. Coping with and adapting to change are fundamental to a
pragmatist perspective (e.g., Johnson, 2007; Schulkin, 1992; Smith,

1970). One major behavioral adaptation we make are the precommitments that we impose on the organization of action as we seek to embrace the precariousness of our existence.

EVOLUTIONARY CONTEXT: NATURE ALIVE. The concept of the evolutionary tree is itself an evolving scientific and historical issue (Boyd & Richerson, 1985; Gould, 2002; Simpson, 1949, 1961, 1980). The conventional ladderlike schema, representing an ascending hierarchy in which modern humans occupy the ultimate evolutionary niche, has now been replaced with a bush that has many lateral and parallel branches. This revised conceptualization allows for an exploration of the convergence and divergence of branches with regard to other primates, which are near and yet distinct from our own branch. It also allows humans to evaluate our place in nature and, perhaps, to ponder nature.

Evolutionary theory puts into context something about our original condition of knowing. From hunter-gatherer to agrarian and industrial times, humans have tried to lend structure to what they see and to preserve it in some way. Dwelling together led to the sharing of workloads and efficient task completion, which afforded individuals more discretionary time. With this extra time, at some point, someone created a visual representation in the form of a drawing, some of the earliest of which have survived in the deep caves of southwestern Europe. We cannot be certain why these drawings were made, though they could well have been ritualistic charms to secure favorable hunting. These representations likely provided some sense of security and stability in an uncertain world; preservation of the world through visual representation may have reduced anxiety. It may also have been a symbol of wealth or skill, as the artist typically boasted in the drawings of successful kills during the hunt. However, the hunt was not the only subject of these drawings; deities were depicted as icons of rebirth and regrowth, essential features of nature (Bachofen, 1926/1967; Nash, 1967; Oelschlaeger, 1991). It is doubtful

FIGURE 2.1. Looking at animate and inanimate objects (Yansen & Schulkin, 2007).

that early humans had an idea of "art" or decoration, in our contemporary sense, or even that they made distinctions between what was useful and what was decorative. This distinction is really a product of the nineteenth century and the rise of the Industrial Revolution. Michelangelo, for example, would not have made this distinction.

Our ideas about nature have evolved with our culture and our ways of understanding (Collingwood, 1945/1976; Schulkin, 1996). Nature was understood originally as having two primary categories, alive and lifeless (Whitehead, 1938/1967) (see Figure 2.1). More recently, lifelike properties infuse both animate and inanimate elements of the natural world (Oelschlaeger, 1991). A cosmology based on the four elements gave way to lifeless atomism, ethereal forms, mechanical bodies, and back again to animate nature (Emerson, 1855/1883; Whitehead, 1933/1961). Thus, our sense of nature evolves with our understanding and has taken what is, for many, a gratifying turn toward an appreciation of wild places (Nash, 1967). The sensibility of the naturalist (e.g., Thoreau, 1971) pervades the ways in which nature

TABLE 2.1. *Darwin's explanatory model of evolution through natural selection*

Fact 1
Potential exponential
increase of populations
(superfecundity) (*Source:*
Paley, Malthus, Others)

Fact 2
Observed steady-state
stability of populations
(*Source:* universal
observations)

Fact 3
Limitation of resources
(*Sources:* observation
reinforced by Malthus)

Inference 1
Struggle for
existence among
individuals
(*Author:* Malthus)

Fact 4
Uniqueness of the
individual (*Source:*
animal breeders,
taxonomists)

Fact 5
Heritability of much
of the individual
variation
(*Source:* animal
breeders)

Inference 2
Differential
survival; i.e.
natural selection
(*Author:* Darwin)

Inference 3
Through many
generations:
evolution
(*Author:* Darwin)

Source: Mayr, 1991.

is depicted (Midgley, 1979, 1995; Worster, 1979/1991) and can engender an appreciation for the diversity of species (Wilson, 1992).

In the nineteenth and early twentieth centuries, many theorists envisioned evolutionary progress as gradual (Bury, 1933/1960; Huxley, 1863, 1909). It was theorized that as animals progressed at tasks, they became smarter and better adapted to their environments. Each stage in evolution was seen as linked to the past, building slowly and steadily from there. In the process, species transformed and new variants emerged. Table 2.1 depicts the basic characteristics of Darwinian theory (Mayr, 1991).

However, evolution is not always slow and gradual nor necessarily progressive. In fact, change might be radically discontinuous (Goldsmith, 1940/1982; Gould & Eldridge, 1977), indicating a break with preceding events, such as the case of linguistic competence (Humboldt, 1836/1971). The number of genes in the human genome turned out to be much smaller than had been thought, and humans share 98 percent of our genetic code with the other great apes. Although no known precursor exists for syntactic competence in such primates (e.g., Hauser, Chomsky, & Fitch, 2002; Premack & Premack, 1983), most primates are social animals that exhibit gestural responding to keep track of the social milieu and other communicative elaborations, which are significant to evolutionary theory and perhaps to our own linguistic competence (Cheney & Seyfarth, 2007; Corballis, 2002; Dunbar, 1996). Syntactical competence tied to language use is a unique species-specific expression in humans (Chomsky, 1965, 1972; Levinson, 2006; Pinker, 1994).

The development of syntactic expression marked a drastic break with the past because syntax and evolved language use made radical change possible. In hominid evolution, evolutionarily abrupt changes seem to have taken place in the rapid expansion of symbolic expression (Mellars, 1989; Mithen, 1996; Foley, 1995, 1996). Abrupt evolutionary change, like gradual change, may or may not be for the better. In this view, great or small changes may occur over a relatively short period, provoking disequilibrium followed by periods of stasis (Gould & Eldridge, 1977), or so-called punctuated equilibrium (Gould, 2002; Eldridge, 1985, 1990).

AGENCY, CORTICAL FUNCTION, SOCIAL CONTACT. Diverse forms of hominoids, we now know, overlapped and were even in competition with one another, sometimes replacing less adapted species (e.g., Neanderthals; Foley, 2001; Mellars, 1996; Mithen, 1996, 2006). *Homo sapiens* came to dominate the landscape as other humanlike primates became extinct (see Figure 2.2) (Boyd & Richerson, 2005; Foley & Lahr, 2003; Mellars, 1996; Mithen, 2006; Tattersall, 1993).

But what emerged, namely *Homo sapiens*, was a highly linguistic, tool-using social animal with an elaborate array of cognitive skills

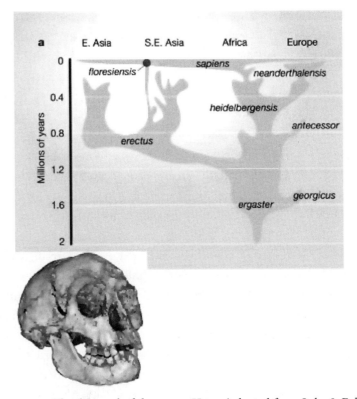

FIGURE 2.2. The dispersal of the genus *Homo* (adapted from Lahr & Foley, 2004).

(Foley & Lahr, 2003). Diverse forms of instrumental expression and tool use arose rapidly, as did varied forms of cognitive expression, some broad and some specific (Mithen, 1996, 2006).

Cognitive expansion across diverse problematic contexts, which develops from narrow adaptive abilities, is a feature of the human mind (Donald, 1991, 2004; Mithen, 1996, 2006; Rozin, 1976). It is the expansion into greater novelty by increased accessibility to the cognitive functions by neural architecture that reflects our evolutionary ascent (Jackson, 1884/1958; Rozin, 1976). A key feature of cognitive expansion is the integration of several orientations to coping with the world: social intelligence, technical abilities, diverse expression of natural knowledge, and language use in more varied and novel contexts (Geschwind, 1974; Mithen, 1996, 2006; Rozin, 1976). Importantly, a wide variety of evidence links the degree of social interaction with neocortical expansion (Aiello & Dunbar, 1993; Dunbar & Schultz, 2007; Mellars, 1989).

Visual binocularity is associated in primates with brain expansion (Barton, 2004, 2006); importantly, the larger and more diverse are the forms of social interaction, the greater is the degree of corticalization of function (Barton, 2006; Dunbar, 2007). In other words, diverse models of group size have been linked to neocortical enlargement (Dunbar & Shultz, 2007) and cognitive competence (Byrne, 1995; Byrne & Corp, 2004); cognitive systems, however, are distributed across the neural axis (Barton, 2006; Schulkin, 2004).

The degree of cognitive competence and social gesture, bipedal organization, communicative engagement, diverse tool use, and pedagogy is clearly linked to an expansion of the range of social contact (Corballis & Lea, 1999; Dunbar, 2003; Foley, 1996; Gibson & Ingold, 2003; Jolly, 1966, 1999). The greater is the social contact, the greater is the tendency toward increased cortical mass (Barton, 2006; Byrne & Corp, 2004; Dunbar & Schultz, 2007). For example, the more grooming-related behavioral responses, reconciliation, and social contact, the greater is the degree of neocortical expansion (see Figure 2.3). This may be particularly pronounced in females, for whom social contact is obviously linked to reproduction (Jolly, 1966, 1999).

The important point in the evolution of *Homo sapiens* is the combination of deception, trust, and cooperation as important cognitive and regulatory adaptations (Jolly, 1966, 1999). Competition is often overstated at the expense of cooperation; we readily cooperate, and it is in our short- and long-term interests to do so often. With corticalization of function came the ability to regulate the diverse competing social interests that interact with different motivational systems (Swanson, 2000).

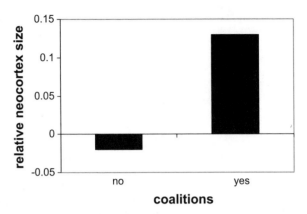

FIGURE 2.3. Relative neocortex size in species that do and do not form coalitions with other group members (solitary and monogamous species excluded) (Dunbar & Schultz, 2007).

UNDERSTANDING AND EVOLUTION. Evolutionary theory is filled with gaps and perhaps more speculation than would be comfortable in other scientific contexts. The gaps, however, fit within the bounds of other evidence in the biological sciences (e.g., genes) that links humans to earlier species. Nonetheless, evolutionary considerations are the background theory (Dobzhansky, 1962). Thus, there is some evidence, including fossils, tools, and skeletons, that more than one modern form of the human species populated the earth at the same time, competing and perhaps cooperating for survival. Modern evolutionary theory thus provides a basic heuristic framework within which biological activity is instantiated and viewed from a coherent perspective (Mayr, 1942/1982, 1963). That there are discontinuities within this framework may be due to our limited knowledge or may be a reflection of the fact that the process of evolution is typified by breaks followed by periods of stasis (Goldsmith, 1940/1982; Gould, 2002; Gould & Eldridge, 1977). Not every feature of a biological entity is an adaptation (Gould & Lewontin, 1979), and adaptive arguments must be viewed with caution, as they too often become circular. Table 2.2 depicts one time framework for human evolution.

TABLE 2.2. *Approximate timeline for the succession of hominids*

Time before present	Event	Characteristics
5 million years	Hominid line and chimpanzee split from common ancestor	
4 million years	Oldest known australopithecine	• Erect posture • Shared food • Division of labor • Nuclear family structure • Large number of children • Longer weaning period
2 million years	Oldest known habilines	• As above, with crude cutting tools • Variable but larger brain size
1.5 million years	*Homo erectus*	• Much larger brain • More elaborate tools • Migration out of Africa • Seasonal base camps • Use of fire, shelters
300,000 years	*Homo sapiens*	• Second major increase in brain size • Anatomy of vocal tract begins to assume modern form
50,000 years	Modern humans	

Source: Adapted from Donald, 1991.

Evolutionary theorizing requires careful observation amid a core set of concepts (e.g., speciation, natural selection) that have determined the meaning of evolution. It is rich in unresolved disputes, such as whether language evolved from gestures or from vocalization (see Corballis, 2002; Pinker, 1994). The current prevalent conception of evolution is historical and teaches about fluid process, that the world is not stagnant. We no longer regard evolution as tantamount to progress. Devolution of function, a neurological term for the breakdown of the brain, is as real as is evolution of neural function (Jackson, 1884/1958). The rate of change can be abrupt, as when a state of disequilibrium is reached and new adaptive and innovative solutions are generated. Both evolution and history are testimony to abrupt change, which is not always for the better.

From Aristotle to Darwin, we have come to use categories to understand the changes of living things (Johanson & Edey, 1981; Leakey, 1934/1954; Leakey & Lewin, 1977; Moore, 1993). Nature's purpose, though not intentional, is expressed in wondrous functional adaptations. Great spectacles of awesome beauty and expression can be found everywhere. The events of nature are time dependent and history bound. Time frame considerations are for understanding our evolution: Table 2.3 depicts another recent view of our evolutionary history from Africa (Mellars, 2006).

Note that agriculture emerged about ten thousand years ago and written language approximately five thousand years ago (Mithen, 1996, 2006). This is quite recent when put in perspective. More ancient is our orientation to detect something different and unexpected; what underlies our cognitive architecture is the detection of uncertain and discrepant events, which also underlies inquiry (Dewey 1925/1989; Peirce, 1878).

UNCERTAINTY, DISCREPANCY, PREDICTION, INQUIRY. The familiar-unfamiliar distinction is as fundamental a cognitive distinction in the organization of action as is the animate-inanimate distinction (Keil, 1987; Rozin, 1976). Cognitive distinctions involve human expectations and extend to the diverse ways in which we explore the world. They are fundamentally linked with how humans placate fears of what we know and do not know. In part, mythological discourse developed, like visual representation, to quiet our fears and uncertainties. But myths and storytelling served to do more than help us to cope with uncertainty. They also served to teach, deify, ritualize, and give memory a social embodiment (Atran 1990/1996; Sperber 1975, 1985).

Visual representation provided a sense of control, of mastery over nature. Both tools and art were used for understanding. The brains of early humans evolved as they engaged the world around them. Today,

TABLE 2.3. *Human population dispersal from Africa.*
Adapted from Mellars, 2006.

150,000–200,000 before present (BP) Initial emergence of anatomically and genetically modern populations in Africa

↓

110,000–90,000 BP Temporary dispersal of anatomically modern populations (with Middle Palaeolithic technology) from Africa to southwest Asia, associated with clear symbolic expression

↓

80,000–70,000 BP Rapid climatic and environmental changes in Africa

↓

80,000–70,000 BP Major technological, economic and social changes in southern and eastern Africa

↓

70,000–60,000 BP Major population expansion in Africa from small source area

↓

ca. 60,000 BP

Dispersal of modern populations from Africa to Eurasia

if no problems are in sight, many humans create their own problems
and conjure up new things about which to worry. We seem to need
to struggle, and thus our nervous systems invent phantoms. But we
do not have to create phantoms very often, for the world makes its
presence known (see Figure 2.4).

FIGURE 2.4. Fearful events.

The most evolved parts of the central nervous system, such as the cortex, serve as constructive organs and create ideational influences that in turn create arenas for fantasized action. We create and model the environment to which we adapt, though that does not guarantee that the representations are simple copies of the environment (e.g., Godfrey-Smith, 1996).

The brain evolved to create and organize action, but at times it runs rampant with aberrant results. Perhaps the root of the chaos lies in our developmental past: the legacy of the traumas of our early life in child-hood compounded with our biological inheritance. Early trauma, in conjunction with daily exposure to the ambiguities of everyday life, can lead one to search for certain things that might go wrong. The unease that is built into us has to do with the fact that if we were wrong about a predator stalking the water hole, life was over; there was no second chance. Bad events were dangerous – so much so that vig-ilance toward danger was perhaps more important than attention to good. This may be why there seem to be more negative emotions than positive ones, and why it is easier for us to recall negative events. They have prominence and importance in our evolutionary past, because it was imperative to learn quickly what was bad or harmful (e.g., food sources; Rozin, 1976; Rozin & Schulkin, 1990).

It should not be surprising that a significant portion of our brains is oriented toward detecting discrepancy, noticing uncertainty, and cap-turing stability (Dewey, 1925/1989; Kagan, 2002) After all, a common feature of our experience is pervaded by this sense of the world and the categories of thought that make coherent action possible. Some individuals have a greater response to unfamiliar events; for exam-ple, socially shy individuals are more responsive to unfamiliar social contexts (Kagan, 1984, 2002). But this broad-based response, caution in the face of the unfamiliar, is an important cognitive/behavioral adaptation that underlies human social behaviors.

The detection of a discrepancy in expected events results in greater activity to ameliorate the discrepancy by investigation and learning (Dewey, 1925/1989; Loewenstein, 1994; Peirce, 1878; Rescorla & Wagner, 1972). In other words, a core pragmatist perspective is that inquiry occurs with the breakdown of expectations of outcomes, a devolution of coherence of behavioral options. A broad array of learning, through new problem-solving search principles, occurs when expectations are thwarted. Of course, inquiry is more than this, but the disruption of expectations is a core feature of the organization of learning and inquiry.

Moreover, the prediction of behavioral events is a core cognitive feature and not simply the association of events in learning and inquiry. An important discovery is that there is a set of learning equations that are not coupled with contingencies, and time of occurrence is not an axiomatic factor in learning per se but rather a function for predicting events (Rescorla & Wagner, 1972). This view of inquiry and learning was prescient, for the variants of this view would capture learning theory through what became known as the Rescorla-Wagner equation:

$$\Delta V = \alpha\beta(\lambda - V)$$

The Rescorla-Wagner equation depicts the associative strengths of stimuli and how these discrepancies from expectations are resolved. An association, and thereby learning, occurs by the strength of the predictions that are being developed. The model then not simply becomes a mathematical approach to neural science but also incorporates a cognitive point of view. In the equation, V represents the current associative strength of the stimulus, and λ shows the maximum associative strength of the primary motivating event. The salience of conditioned and unconditioned stimuli is represented by α and β, respectively. The predictability of the primary motivating event is shown in the $(\lambda - V)$ term. When the current and maximum associative strengths of the stimulus are equal, the conditioned stimulus fully predicts the reinforcer. However, when the term is positive (e.g., when λ is greater than V), the associative strength increases and the conditioned stimulus does not fully predict the reinforcer – there is room for learning or inquiry to occur. With increased associative strength, learning will occur, and in fact only occurs when the conditioned stimulus does not entirely predict the event. In contrast, a negative

($\lambda - V$) term occurs when there is a loss of associative strength, and the prediction fails. General informational search and discrepancy mechanisms, the breakdown of established habits of action, underlie our sense of learning and inquiry.

Experiments in both animals and humans reinforce the fact that violation of expectations promotes learning. Indeed, studies of decision making suggest that humans actively search for ways to reduce informational uncertainty (Dewey, 1929/1960; Loewenstein, 1994, 2006) (see Figure 2.5).

In experiments in which parts of a body were presented to subjects and they were asked to guess the person's age, it was found that the ability to fill in the informational gap by the parts shown was positively correlated with curiosity and uncertainty (Loewenstein, 1996, unpublished observations) (see Figure 2.5).

Although uncertainty and insecurity are found in the minds of many animals struggling to survive in nature, humans evolved intricate thoughts about this uncertainty. A core feature of our cognitive arsenal is knotted to the detection of danger. The same is true in many other species, but we are the ones who have a language (and linguistic usage) to express our uncertainty and insecurity, and in an elaborate manner. One might be prepared to accept that higher mammals, such as dolphins, apes, or monkeys, reflect on their experiences in some fashion. They certainly have evolved advanced conceptual frameworks for functioning in the world and for communicating with one another (Marler, 1961; Smith, 1977; Hauser, 2000). When considering animals and whether they experience angst, one should look at their style of existence (e.g., whether they have other animals to fear), whether they have the limbic regions of the brain – the part of the brain that responds to uncertainty – and their behavioral responses, which are sometimes similar to our own (LeDoux, 1996; Rosen & Schulkin, 1998; Schmidt & Schulkin, 1999).

Different regions of the brain are activated when an event becomes uncertain (e.g., Schultz, 2002, 2004). This activity manifests itself

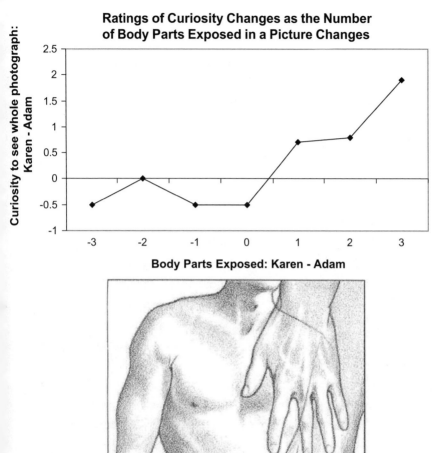

Ratings of Curiosity Changes as the Number of Body Parts Exposed in a Picture Changes

Curiosity to see whole photograph: Karen - Adam

Body Parts Exposed: Karen - Adam

FIGURE 2.5. Kinds of body parts used in the Loewenstein experiment. Subjects were shown zero to three pictures each of parts of a man (Adam) and a woman (Karen). They were then asked to rate how curious they were to see a picture of the whole person on a five-point scale. The vertical scale is the difference in rated curiosity between seeing the picture of Karen and the picture of Adam. The horizontal axis is the difference in the number of pictures of body parts the subject saw between Karen and Adam. In general, a subject was more curious to see the picture of the whole person if they saw more pictures of that person's body parts (Loewenstein, 1999).

across the neocortex, diverse limbic regions in the phylogenetic older cortex (amygdala; LeDoux, 1996; Rosen & Schulkin, 1998; Dolan, 2007), basal ganglia, and brain-stem sites. These neural sites detect and then help prepare the appropriate behavioral responses following the detection of uncertainty (Schultz, 2002). For example, in macaques, there are two classes of neuronal populations; one is knotted to the prediction of reward and its reliability, and the other is tied to failed expectations, both of which figure into the organization of behavior. The central neurotransmitter dopamine is, importantly, knotted to whether the reward is predictable, as this transmitter is vital to the organization of action. Many of these neural sites are below the cortex, and linked to the basal ganglia function, an area of the brain that underlies the integration of sensorimotor function (see Figure 2.6). Different regions of the cortex, particularly frontal and cingulate cortices, are also connected to the prediction of rewards (e.g., Schultz, 2002, 2004).

A wide array of human brain imaging studies have documented that the regions of the frontal cortex are tied to uncertainty, to uncertain expectations. More specifically, studies have shown that the greater are the uncertainty or violations of expectations, the greater is the activation of the frontal and cingulate cortex (e.g., Critchley et al., 2000; Critchley et al., 2003). Uncertainty is often linked to risk and arousal, and these measures are linked to the activation of these cortical sites (Critchley, 2005; Paus, 2001). Conversely, contexts that tend to decrease autonomic expression also tend to decrease responses to uncertainty (Damasio, 1996, 1999).

Uncertainty is as basic as it is regulatory; an important adaptation is the recognition of these facts. Humans with evolved brains ponder the meaning of things, hypothesize, and then generate explanations that are cumulative, elaborated, extended, and sometimes discarded. The uncertainty of life powerfully drives people to make sense of events, understand, conquer, or simply accept or deny them. The uncertainty of the present and the underlying insecurity that it

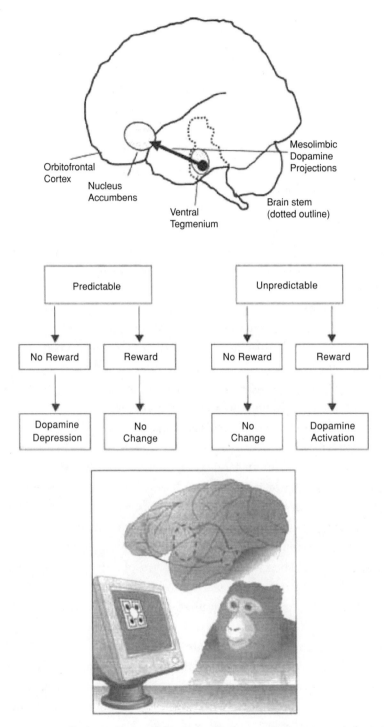

FIGURE 2.6. Brain regions and dopamine tied to predicting events (adapted from Schultz, 2002).

generates pushes people to anticipate and plan ahead, to prepare for
what is to come, and to want to control the course of events.

PERMANENCE AND CHANGE: AGENCY, ADAPTATION, HUMAN EXPE-
RIENCE. The desire to control our life events implies that we believe
ourselves to be agents of change (Dewey, 1929/1960). Since the beginning of civilization, humans have often speculated about the prospects
of change: coding it, remembering it, adapting to it. For Heraclei-
tus, the Greek philosopher, change was endemic and at the heart of
being in the world. For Parmenides, another significant Greek thinker,
change was a disaster and the beginning of degradation; as he put it,
"reality is motionless" (Kirk & Raven, 1957). For some later thinkers,
all that was worthy was permanent and not subject to the changing
tides of events. All that was true was eternal and fixed. For other
philosophers, the flux of life was a river of uncharted courses, where
staying afloat amid the turbulence was difficult, and many drowned.
The cognitive poles were omnipresent fluidity and eternal stability. For anyone seeking a net of safety, permanence would seem the
best choice. Safety, after all, motivates many human choices, such as
dwelling, labor, and marriage partners.

   As has been mentioned, one cognitive and practical way humans
explore the new is by flavoring it with the old, the familiar. Humans
often do this as we try new foods (Rozin, 1976, 1998) and name
new places (e.g., New England, New Amsterdam). Naming objects –
marking them and keeping track of them over time – is a fundamental
feature of linguistic expression and a form of cognitive adaptation
(e.g., Kripke, 1980; Putnam, 1990).

   The tension between the familiar and the unfamiliar underlies a
basic psychobiological fact: one tends to stay with the familiar until
forced into new territory (see Figure 2.7). One might sample what is
new but only from the purview of the familiar, the accustomed. The
promise of permanence is more alluring than is the risk of uncertainty.

   In contrast, for classical pragmatists, experience is not passive
(Godfrey-Smith, 1996; Hendel, 1959; Smith, 1985). The mind is

FIGURE 2.7. Keeping things the same while exploring something different (Yansen & Schulkin, 2007).

construed in active terms in which cognitive adaptation and tracking events into coherence are primary activities. Transactions with the world, the testing of ideas, self-corrective hypothesis testing, are what predominate a normative set of goals – at least ideally. What packs experience with a punch are the goals as they are being pursued; motivation is endemic in action. Thought is embodied in action and is not a spectator in the stands. Truth may be what is agreed upon, contingently, by a community of inquirers, or what settles over time, but in the give-and-take Dewey suggested that we live with "warranted assertions" (Dewey, 1938). Reason is demythologized to adaptation and to shorter-term purposes (e.g., Cherniak, 1986; Clark, 2003; Gigerenzer, 2007; Kornblith, 1993; Simon, 1962, 1982). We accept that reason must be bounded by circumstance and good sense. We look to satisfy and not necessarily always to optimize our decisions; the tools we use to reach this point are instrumental and heuristic in nature (Baron, 1985, 1988/2008; Simon, 1982).

As is inevitable, change takes place, including scientific change from experiment and experience. These changes were basic to the new sciences that evolved in the early modern era – the romantic vision of science liberated from the Scholasticism and rationalization of the past. A philosophy of change became prominent in the nineteenth and twentieth centuries. The cultural air was rich in evolutionary theorizing (Eiseley, 1959/1961; Himmelfarb, 1959/1962). Charles Darwin's grandfather, Erasmus Darwin (physician, poet, naturalist, evolutionist) wrote tomes in bequest to evolution, an appreciation of objects in nature (1789/1991, 1794/1801). Nature was alive (e.g., Coleridge, 1840/1956; see King-Hele, 1986) and full of uncertainty and the precarious. Voyages to distant lands were idealized and realized; the voyage of the HMS *Beagle*, on which Darwin encountered seminal experiences in South America and the South Pacific, was just one of many such ventures sparking new perspectives.

Other conceptions of change emerged through biology as the Aristotelian order of biological rigidity was replaced with biological fluidity. The static order of nature was undermined by the developing intellectual perspective that envisioned an evolving planet. This development first emerged in physics, with theories like the nebula hypothesis explaining the origins of the universe. Then, within biology, there developed an evolutionary sense; no longer was order rigidly ordained until eternity. Animal life evolved, competed, and survived or extinguished. Change lay bare at the plane of evolving life: species evolved by excelling in some functions and losing other functions.

Our sense of nature evolved as human intellectual organs and culture evolved, and as people realized that we were as much a part of nature as we were of culture (Nash, 1967; Oelscheager, 1991; Ruse, 2006; Schulkin, 1996). Early in our evolutionary ascent, we were one small part of nature. As we struggled to cope, we sought to capture the shapes and sounds of the nature we were experiencing.

The conception of nature, a real sense of reproductive and regenerative properties inherent in biological events, was often expressed in myth. This is linked to what Bachofen, a nineteenth-century political historian, called "mother right," a sense of matriarchy or "generative power of matter" (1926/1967, p. 98).

What is apparent in all of these events is a deep-seated sense of core cognitive orientation toward biological events that captures biological change (Keil, 1979, 1983, 1992; Wilson, 2005). Humans bear an autonomous set of predilections for the purpose of categorizing biological kinds, including (1) reproductive faculties, (2) some form of internal structure, (3) developmental trajectory, (4) core and stable features over time, (5) essential features that capture more than sensory properties, (6) trajectories that indicate purpose, or teleological expectations, and (7) properties that are inherent in the natural kind and that are linked to other objects. Nature is perceived as beautiful, awful, awesome, and peaceful (e.g., Kant 1792/1951; Whitehead, 1938/1967). As we do, our conceptions of nature evolve. Nature is alive and booming with activity and expression.

TAMING DISCOMFORT: PRECOMMITMENTS, PLANNING AHEAD. With the evolution of our conception of nature, we have come to recognize the uncertainty that exists within it. Our planning is an attempt to stabilize the future as well as to control and predict it (Dewey, 1925/ 1989; Elster, 1979/1988). The delight we feel in planning is considered a healthy psychological feature.

In a precarious world, little is safe and secure, and planning in itself is, in part, a risk. If all planning were for the safe and the secure, dead habit would be the result. Because we need to allow for both spontaneity and the forms of regularity that guide us, humans pursue an element of risk as we move ahead. Stability and adventure are intermingled. Risk remains basic, even pleasurable, but we taper it; some of us go on fast rides at amusement parks that look risky but are typically safe (Rozin & Fallon, 1987).

Expectations serve to ground and relieve the discomfort of uncertainty and risk but sometimes may exacerbate it. As we plan ahead, the familiar guides us. More than this, however, expectations are the thread of planning ahead. Our expectations – our goals – guide us and are instrumental to how we envision our future.

Of necessity, we live with the fear and uncertainty that coexist with the acquired stability of laying plans (Dewey, 1925/1989, 1929/1960). While continuing to act, we search for new reasons for action. It is imperative to avoid paralysis, lethargy, and negativism in response to the fear and uncertainty of the future. It is easy to declare futility, but fortune is one of the unexpected joys in life. In planning, we must be responsive to the vector of possibilities and to the unexpected. Thus, if our planning is so rigid as to preclude novelty, life falters myopically. The sense of horizons opens with fortune. Fortuna is hard and heartfelt, not magic. There is also the luck of the muses as life turns in the direction that it does. Although there is no doubt an element of luck, fortune almost always is derived from labor. At times Fortuna gives us a great gift – a piece of grace, a surprise that resonates in an appreciative mind.

Keeping perspective on all this is hard to do – impossible for some, difficult for almost all. Yet the lure of the future helps to call us forward. Causation, in this regard, is not simply from the past; the future pulls seductively. The present is "specious," as James (1890/1917) suggested. It is extended as it receives the pushes of the past and the pulls of the future. But the past lingers powerfully, and the backward pull of the familiar placates. Past comforts ameliorate present fears; nostalgia calls us back. As we plan ahead, perhaps one of the key features is the consideration of our commitments (Elster, 1979/1988), which represent the practices that guide us through life (Bourdieu, 1980/1990), as well as of our beliefs and desires (Hirshman, 1982).

This future orientation reveals our intentional stance: the teleological. Our commitments organize what we do, what we strive for, what we allow as possible to pursue. To reduce conflict, perhaps, we limit our choices, but seemingly paradoxically, for by this act we open up further possibilities. We reduce our options of what we envision as possible and impose upon ourselves rules of coherence (see Figure 2.8). For example, we remove ourselves from the people and places that may be deleterious, or we surround ourselves with those that are cheerful and positive. We commit ourselves and set a course of action with the decision to diet, to parent, to fulfill a job, to exercise, or to be faithful in marriage. Such commitments are at the basis of everyday action and organize a purposeful life.

Such commitments are the acts of social life, serving as both the pushes and the pulls. They push us in a particular direction, and we are pulled toward the goal at the same time. Precommitments are essential to organizing what we do (Elster, 1979/1988). They provide order for our experience, even when what we are experiencing seems irrational, such as the hunger involved in losing weight. Commitments stabilize us, and establish the necessity of actions as we prepare for what is to come.

As Elster has suggested, behavioral adaptations may include the following:

1. Reducing options
2. Imposing costs
3. Establishing rewards
4. Creating timelines
5. Tagging preferences
6. Investing in bargaining
7. Reducing knowledge
8. Enhancing certain passions

FIGURE 2.8. Ulysses and the binding of behavior toward the future.

Although commitments bind us to pursue certain activities despite the inherent regularity that we encounter, insecurity and uncertainty linger. The future is always unknown, and an element of uncertainty is pervasive. To lump all that matters into the present is to impoverish the present and reduce it to a transient moment. An appreciation of the present is one thing; to make it all of life is quite another. At moments of extreme crisis, the present can seem overwhelming; its scope is breadthless and without dimensions. In normal life, the present is lived with the twin promises of planned goals and past experience. When one plans ahead, one seeks a balance of regularity and spontaneity. When dead habits predominate, the habits surely deprive one of spontaneity, of creative novelty, and of new goals. Nevertheless, whole communities may find refuge in habits, often when under stress, such as viewing cinema during the Depression or praying during war. Such habits are not bad; they serve as pressure valves.

PRAGMATIC COHERENCE AND ADAPTATION. Past regularity is essential and serves as the bedrock of order and coherent experience. Dewey described what he called "funded knowledge," in which truth is the cumulative wisdom of past experience. One does not discard this wisdom but instead uses it for guidance while engaging the present and planning for the future. To eliminate the past to romantic oblivion or to overextend it into causal sterility is obviously too aberrant. A balanced vision prepares us for what is to come and stretches the past into the present amid the pulls of the future and the expressions of the present.

The vision of the present is one of actions, of events under way; it is a healthy actualization of human capabilities. We start from movement, engagement, and interaction; we do not start learning or preparing for the future from a fixed starting point. There are, perhaps, few a priori starting points, except for those that address the structure of mind and culture. We are not static but theory driven, centrifugal (in the vernacular of neuroscience), and anticipatory.

Thinking and action are embodied in preparation for the future. The connective nature of the activity is unique and refreshing. Planning necessitates a flexibility of mind. It means that one changes one's views as new data become available. This is no easy task. We often look away and do not acknowledge what is contrary to our expectations.

This is where a blend of balanced ontological insecurity with episte-mological uncertainty can orient one toward perceiving the possible and encourage one not to look away from contrary data. How we use the resources of our environment is a consideration in planning ahead.

Planning ahead teaches us to distinguish between short- and long-term agendas, because short-term modifications are inadequate for long-term issues. This is particularly true as one envisions one's life, what one would like to be, how one structures one's life, one's time frame, one's conceptions of future selves. Planning ahead is also essen-tial to how one relates to others, including those about whom one cares. The same is also true of environmental and economic planning.

Planning permeates human life. As we plan ahead, we enlarge our notion of what it means to belong to a community. A future-oriented conception is one in which the vision of being in the world is not of an individual isolated from the environment but of an individual within an environment and a community. A community transcends national borders to some extent. The vision is one of nested and networked communities, individuals locating themselves in communities and building new ones.

We plan for what is to come, and we wait for the unexpected out-pouring of what is out there to be encountered. The prudent recourse is to stretch the good as far as it can go and to hope for the best. Good fortune might prevail for extended moments, stretching a life that has more good than bad. Good things emerge by fortune and labor, but labor mostly comes first. Fortune often rains on those who labor hard and with good sense.

CONCLUSION. As insecurity and uncertainty are basic to animal life, so too are risk and adventure. We have evolved a set of cognitive predilections that focus on animate objects, on other possible expe-riences, on the sense of agency. We venture out toward new arenas of discourse. We enjoy novelty; we are attracted to and pursue new terrain. The lure of different lands, for example, pulls us to sojourn in new places. The roads are unfamiliar as are the faces and cultures, and at times there is danger. Although in its extreme forms the pursuit of danger can be pathological, the acceptance of risk and the ensuing thrill are part of the pleasure of travel. Risk must be not only accepted but also welcomed, for many worthy things necessitate risk as part of the adventure and the pursuit. Risk is felt. It is exciting. It is motivating. It can also be aversive and frightening.

As we plan ahead, what we often face is a state of anxiety or worry. Adaptation is a constant feature of forging coherence and of trying to achieve some semblance of peacefulness. Some worries motivate and some worries diminish life, and the border between healthy and afflicted worry can sometimes be imperceptible. It is hard enough to put on one's shoes in the morning without being reminded of our daily worries. When worry predominates pathologically, we go nowhere; we remain stuck and immobile. Psychological death threatens to draw us downward. Thus, because insecurity and uncertainty are forever present, worry is an ontological part of being. Our brains try to tame uncertainty and adapt to the insecurity that pervades human experience (Dewey, 1925/1989).

Existential angst serves, in part, as an initiative to plan ahead. But then so do competing and striving for what is just beyond our grasp, continuing to dream as we proceed into the future. We stretch the present and are mindful of the past as we move ahead. But sometimes the steps ahead are radical; large leaps acknowledge the risks and the limits of our reason. Machiavelli may not have been far off in emphasizing that fortune conquers by the force of our actions. We can prepare for change not only by thinking ahead but by returning to the past as well.

We live with worry in the search for knowledge, surprised by the unexpected and humbled by the daily reminder of our limitations. A real but frail historical sense of progressivism runs through intellectual discourse within a sense of self-corrective vulnerable inquiry.

Planning ahead, along with forming alliances to acquire territory and food, figure importantly in our evolutionary development. Concurrent with the abrupt expansion of symbolic expression were rapid technological advances. As are evolutionary changes, economic and technological changes are often abrupt and have a far-reaching impact as their dramatic effects break from the equilibrium of the past (Elster, 1983/1988). Many classical pragmatists (e.g., Peirce, 1878), emphasize disequilibrium, or the breakdown of habits, as a facilitator of change.

Stability is an achievement, as is the uncovering of novelty. But in a real sense we are historical creatures, thrown out into a world (Heidegger, 1927/1962) in which we have to adapt, generate a coherent plan, and fit into a social milieu (or not), in which a sense of agency rich in history matters. Humanity began, in part, with representations like the ones in caves and rock art, trying to capture awe-inspiring nature alive, with concepts like animacy and agency tied to a fragile though evolving humanization. Through understanding we were attempting to both know and placate our fears and our existential concerns. We were also trying to anchor them in time.

3

Time and Memory: Historical Sensibilities

Therefore am I still
A lover of the meadows and the woods,
And mountains; and of all that we behold
From this green earth; of all the mighty world
Of eye, and ear, – both what they half create,
And what perceive...
  – William Wordsworth, "Lines Composed a
  Few Miles above Tintern Abbey"

We are historical animals. We pass time, and codify it for endless use. Humans not only use the innate clocks endogenous to our biological system but also expand them to the ontological condition of being part of the larger world. The background for historical sensibility is grounded in our evolutionary past, with the problem-solving tool-boxes that underlie both our evolutionary and our cultural pasts. Consider the psychological and neurological mechanisms of memory that underlie our historical sensibility.

William James (1890/1917) understood that memory, like consciousness, is not a thing but a set of adaptive functions. However, one of the more dubious distinctions is that between cognitive and noncognitive systems in memory; procedural or episodic memory is no less cognitive than declarative or semantic memory. It may be less complex, have fewer inferences, and so on, but one side is not noncognitive and the other cognitive. These are all information systems carried by the brain. Making this point does not discount the important differences in these systems, some of which reach an awareness level and are more transparent (declarative memory versus procedural systems: knowing how to do something versus knowing that I know how I know to do something; Mishkin, 1984; Ryle, 1949; Squire, 1987).

From keeping track of when events occur to coding the intervals between events (Gallistel, 1990), time is a fundamental part of our psychobiological hardware. At our core, we are historical; basic clock mechanisms set the stage for historical sensibility. An evolved brain is the basis of historical consciousness. Historical revelation is tied to the mechanisms by which time and memory are integrated. More evolved neural networks organize the temporal regulation of experience and behavior.

Historical sensibility is tied to our sense of time – the biological clocks, tagging day and night and seasonal changes, that are internally generated but that evolved in the context of real-world cognitive and physiological adaptations (Buzsaki, 2006; Gallistel, 1990). A conception of time is fundamental to central nervous system function (Gallistel, 1990). One common way in which to understand the spontaneity of animal action is to examine the diverse endogenous clocks that generate action. We experience the world in causal terms (Bergson, 1919/1946; James, 1890, 1917; Whitehead, 1927/1953); our sense of agency is knotted to the generation of spontaneous actions.

As Collingwood (2001) noted, "history like science starts from experience" (p. 135). Experience is the appreciation of other lives, of agents struggling to persevere (see also Cassirer, 1953/1957). History pervades all forms of human life and begins with cognitive systems in which various forms of memory play an important role in the regulation of behavior. The rudiments of history begin with our sense of time (e.g., Dilthey, 1926/1961; Gibbon, 1788/1952; Hacking, 1999a; Jaspers, 1949/1968; Lovejoy, 1955; Lukas, 1968/1977, Lowith, 1949, Machiavelli, 1525/1988).

This chapter discusses time, memory, facilitation of memory, and the brain. It then moves to the human sense of history. Our sense of history is replete with purposive action, the accounts one provides for coherent action with purpose, over time and rooted in place and space. The common theme is that historical sensibility should be expressed in every discipline. The historical sense reflects the cultures in which we live. I suggest that some goals of a historical sensibility are to provide a prophylactic against abuse toward others and an existential sense of how we got here and to be humbled by a sense of self-corrective inquiry.

BIOLOGICAL CLOCKS AND TIME. A sense of history is an innate human proclivity (Gazzaniga, 1998) and an important endowment not shared by most other animals. Birds may sing in similar dialects, dolphins may interact socially, chimpanzees may express warlike territorial similarities, but none has the sense for history that we humans do. Historical sensibility is an important human adaptation to inherent uncertainty.

Biological clocks in plants and insects are well represented in reptiles, birds, and mammals (Bunning, 1963). Cyclic internal machinations and the external landscape are coordinated into an expression of adaptation. But the internal environment is separate from the external environment. Active self-regulation lies at the heart of our evolutionary landscape. These biological clocks order human experiences as well.

We can be acutely aware of time. But whether or not we are consciously aware of it, the vast cognitive arsenal that underlies behavioral adaptation presupposes sets of timing and memory systems that create a sense of history, both personal and collective. Time, again, is expanded in space: the "specious present" to use a phrase from James (1890/1917; see also Levinson, 1996, 2003; Matlock, 2004) that speaks of how space and time influence each other, of how space is used in

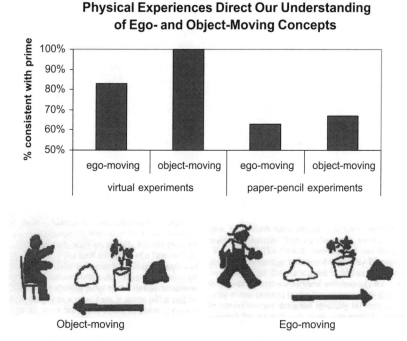

FIGURE 3.1. Subjects in a virtual-reality computer environment (a better simulation of motion than paper-pencil tests or two-dimensional video games) were more likely to act consistently with a spatial prime (adapted from Alloway et al., 2006).

the consideration of time, such as a long and short vacation at a place (Casasanto & Boroditsky, 2008).

Experience and language influence our sense of moving through space, of projecting ahead. That is, one's sense of time is influenced not only by space but also by movement (Alloway, Corley, & Ramscar, 2006; Levinson, 1996) (see Figure 3.1). Perhaps not surprisingly, our sense of motion or physical sensibility affects our sense of time and space. So there is a bodily component of our sense of time and memory of events, which is rich in sensorimotor experiences (Boroditsky & Ramscar, 2002; Glenberg, 1997) and in agency and action (Boroditsky & Ramscar, 2002; Matlock et al., 2004).

Societies vary with regard to their time sensibility (Levinson, 1996, 2003). Moreover, physical gestures and the cultural development of clocklike objects (e.g., calendars) also vary with culture and language. That said, Kant (1787/1965) was not misguided when he asserted that space and time are fundamental categories in the organization of human experience.

PSYCHOBIOLOGY AND CLOCKS. Clocks keep time and, perhaps more important, provide order and coherence. The outer world to which we are trying to adapt requires coherent forms of action. The biological clocks underlying behavior allow us to be anchored to real-world events and to a prized human invention – the many objects made to measure and depict time (Foster & Kreitzman, 2004; Richter, 1965/1979).

Harmonic relationships, as many ancient Greek thinkers understood, represent cycles of events. Cyclic representations have a long history. Prior to the modern era, the understanding of events as cyclic was common. With the advent of Darwinism, fitness and long-term survival became linked to cyclic events. The first biological revolution was then at hand, which manifested as the Darwinian conceptions of adaptation, speciation, secondary sexual characteristics, and problem solving. Animals had been understood as machines, albeit purposeful machines. This machinery, however, reflected variations in design and niche.

Nature selected the features of good fit. Diverse adaptation was part of the machinery expressed in nature. One key feature that facilitates activity and inactivity in many animals is the light-dark cycle (see Figure 3.2). A recurrent feature of the real world, though not everywhere in it, are changes in light levels. The external fact of the sun rising and setting represents objects in the world that root our cognitive resources in real-world events (Barsalou, 2008; Gibson, 1966). This fact is reflected in part by internal neural systems.

FIGURE 3.2. Clocks and seasons (Yansen & Schulkin, 2007).

DAILY ENDOGENOUS CLOCKS. Circadian clocks orient and synchronize an animal's adaptive behavioral and physiological responses to periodic changes in the environment. Even in constant darkness, without signals from external events, animals may generate cyclic

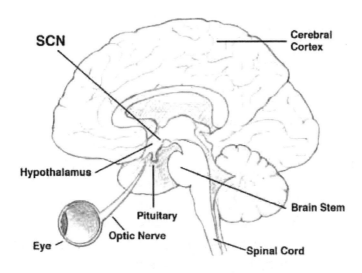

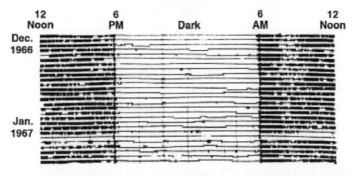

FIGURE 3.3. Regions of the brain, the twenty-four-hour clock, and the running activity of a monkey linked to the twenty-four-hour clock (adapted from Richter, 1965/1979).

rhythmic patterns, both physiological and behavioral (Rosenwasser, 2003). The circadian clock is a fundamental timing device expressed and present in a wide variety of species (Richter, 1965/1979). For example, Figure 3.3 shows the running activity of a monkey, for example, with the lights on or off. A circadian clock contributes importantly to the onset of this behavior (Richter, 1965/1979).

The circadian clock is even expressed in the neonate (Richter, 1965/1979) as an inborn property of his or her nervous system, though psychologically a more evolved sense of time is a necessary precondition for a historical sensibility. Biological clocks are endogenous to the brain and provide animals with the ability to anticipate events in the world – such as when food may become available – so that they can return to places yearly, monthly, weekly, or daily when this might occur (Moore-Ede, Sulzman, & Fuller, 1992; Rosenwasser, 2003).

The circadian clock is used to predict the time of day of reward occurrence, which is important to animals foraging for food, water, or salt (e.g., Rosenwasser, Schulkin, & Adler, 1988; Mistlberger, 1994). In the laboratory, animals such as rats will show anticipatory running before the onset of the actual object that they desire (Rosenwasser et al., 1988). Many different animals in nature, depleted of sodium, actively search for it and ingest it when found. In addition, they remember where it is located (Krieckhaus, 1970) and use a circadian clock to lock in the time of day at which it becomes available. The clock is used to predict events and to orchestrate behavioral and physiological anticipatory adaptive responses. Curt Richter (1965/1979) posited that somewhere in the hypothalamus was a critical site for circadian rhythmicity. This region is now referred to as the suprachiasmatic nucleus of the hypothalamus (e.g., Rosenwasser, 2003).

The circadian clocks influence hormonal secretion. The hormone cortisol, secreted by the adrenal gland, is often referred to as the wake-up hormone. Cortisol is a glucocorticoid hormone that regulates glucose metabolism in cells. It is secreted in greater amounts in the morning, in anticipation of the labor that is about to occur, and secretions decline in the evening (Dallman, 2007; Sapolsky, 1992; 2002; Schulkin, 2003), though this varies depending on what one does at night, such as work or whether one is a nocturnal animal. The important point is that cortisol is, in part, under the influence of circadian rhythmicity and is essential to the organization of behavior and various physiological events.

Time of day and occurrence of opportunities are part of the use of this endogenous clock, but the clock has many different functions. Anticipatory adaptations played a fundamental role in our evolution (Moore-Ede et al., 1992). Richter was prescient in believing that the circadian clock is ancient and even present in single cells. We now know that many end-organ systems in the body (e.g., the liver) have twenty-four-hour rhythms. Richter also suggested the independence of these clocks within different end-organ systems, both within and outside the central nervous system, though damage to a region of the hypothalamus compromises some of these rhythmic patterns.

MULTIPLE CLOCKS. Multiple internal clocks orchestrate behavioral and physiological expression. Richter (1965/1979) and others (Rusak & Zucker, 1979) tagged the importance of the twenty-four-hour clock in a variety of species, noting species variation (e.g., nocturnal animals). A study of individual animals showed some variation in the clocks, under normal conditions, that were further exaggerated under pathological conditions. Richter noted clocks in the Norway rat at 1–2 hours, 24 hours, 4–5 days, 12–14 days, 14–22 days, 30 days, 40–60 days, 76–124 days, and 160–180 days, and some with exceptional duration (e.g., 6.5 years in chipmunks; Richter, 1965/1979; Schulkin, 2005). Richter's emphasis on individual differences, and perhaps his avoidance of statistical analysis, allowed him to pay attention to this variation in clocks perhaps more than others in the field would later do (e.g., circannual rhythms; Nunes, Pelz, Muecke, Holekamp, & Zucker, 2006; Zucker, 1988).

Many studies have demonstrated seasonal clocks that are linked to hibernation and sexual activity. Variations in testosterone and luteinizing hormone concentration, for example, are linked to sexual reproduction activities in spring and summer (Nelson, 1995). Seasonal physiological and behavioral changes in animals are common adaptations. Our ability to detect shifts in season and to anticipate and prepare for those changes are functional adaptations deeply rooted

in our biology (Wingfield, 2004). These clocks organize both behavior and physiology. Some of the mechanisms that generate this sense
are the diverse biological clocks that anchor humans to the world in
which we are trying to adapt (Richter, 1965/1979; Ruby, Dark, Burns,
Heller, & Zucker, 2002).

PSYCHOBIOLOGY, MEMORY, AND THE BRAIN. All temporal systems
probably figure in historical sensibility. In terms of psychology, the key
to historical consciousness is the perception of time and memory –
planning ahead and experiencing the present while coming to terms
with the past (e.g., James, 1890/1917). Memory is not a monolithic
entity. Diverse forms of memory reflect different kinds of tasks, much
as different kinds of intelligence are task specific. Memory systems
are tied to faces, edible objects, places, and so on (Eichenbaum &
Cohen, 2001; Tulving, 2002; Zola & Squire, 2003). Both common and
distinct characterizations of features contribute to the organization of
diverse memory systems (Schacter & Tulving, 1994; Schacter & Addis,
2007).

The mechanisms that organize memory systems are pieces of our
biology that provide coherence and are fundamentally tied to diverse
senses of time. Cognitive systems underlie the encoding of events that
become memory (Baddley, Conway, & Aggleton, 2002; Schacter &
Tulving, 1994). For instance, one memory system is tied to the contingent episodes that underlie our individual experiences, and another
records cultural lexical entries – the larger semantic space that people inhabit and inherit (Tulving, 2002). History, though, is largely a
human phenomenon. As a state of human nature, it has changed our
relationship with the natural world and how we understand ourselves.

As there is no one learning system in the brain (Rozin, 1976), there
are different kinds of memory systems organized within the brain.
These include short- and long-term memory, implicit and explicit
memory, working memory, declarative and procedural memory, and
episodic and semantic memory, all of which exist broadly in our

TABLE 3.1. *A tentative memory taxonomy*

System	Other terms	Subsystems	Retrieval
Procedural	Nondeclarative	Motor skills Cognitive skills Simple conditioning, associative learning	Implicit
Perceptual Representation	Nondeclarative	Visual word, Auditory word from Structural description	Implicit
Semantic	Generic Factual Knowledge	Spatial Relational	Implicit
Primary	Working	Visual Auditory	Explicit
Episodic	Personal Autobiographical Event		Explicit

Source: Schacter & Tulving, 1994.

memory capacity (e.g., Schacter, 1996; Tulving & Craik, 2000) (see Table 3.1). Memory systems link our experiences over time as we imagine ahead (Schacter & Addis, 2007). Learning about other people's experiences is a critical way in which we get a foothold into the world, through education and acculturation.

Procedural and habitual learning are more heavily tied to the basal ganglia, an area of the brain that is itself connected to the organization of action. The hippocampus and the temporal lobe are more linked to declarative memories, which are more conscious to the individual (Mishkin et al., 1984; Squire, 1987, 2004). Some common areas underlie working, episodic, autobiographical, and semantic memory; they include regions of the thalamus, cingulate, frontal and temporal cortex, hippocampus, and amygdala (e.g., Bolhuis, 2000; Squire, 2004). It is autobiographical memory that reflects a sense of agency and our historical predilection.

The hippocampus is involved in short-term memory and the perception of time (Eichenbaum & Cohen, 2001; Squire, 1987; see

Cognitive Adaptation

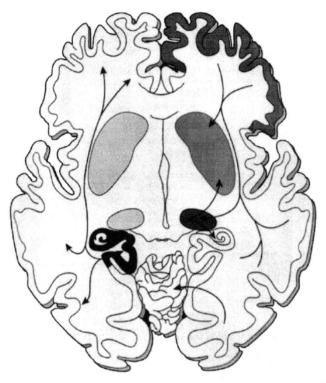

FIGURE 3.4. Many of the brain regions tied to memory including diverse regions of the neocortex, amygdala, hippocampus (Eichenbaum & Cohen, 2001).

Figure 3.4). The amygdala is known for its involvement in memory, particularly those memories that are laden with significance (LeDoux, 1996; Rosen & Schulkin, 1998; Dolan, 2007), such as early and/or formative emotional experiences. These regions of the brain are vital for memories that have emotional significance, that are viscerally represented as something important, something to notice, something to remember. The activation of the frontal neocortex is important in planning ahead and in integrating past experiences (Damasio, 1996, 1999); the parietal cortex is crucial for integrating the ongoing stream of experience, as is the temporal cortex, which is involved in memory. Again, the mechanisms that reflect these diverse memory systems are mostly unconscious. The conscious and unconscious encoding of events reverberates in the brain for long-term consolidation into memory (McGaugh, 2003).

Another form of memory tied to psychobiology is learning about diverse events unrelated to any of our present needs and then using the information at another time when we need a particular source (i.e., latent learning; Tolman, 1949). The vast cognitive organ that is our brain is active unbeknownst to us as it scans and processes diverse kinds of information. For instance, rats in the laboratory can learn where salt is located and how to acquire it at a time when they are not hungry for sodium (Krieckhaus, 1970; Krieckhaus & Wolf, 1968).

Context figures importantly in this phenomenon; the rats are prepared to do more than one thing – something associated with sodium acquisition and something not in their memory for sodium sources – in the absence of sodium hunger. This memory is long lasting and requires only minimal exposure to gustatory signals (Krieckhaus, 1970; Krieckhaus & Wolf, 1968; Schulkin, 1991). In other words, one or two licks at a place associated with sodium are enough for the rats to latently learn something about where the salt is and how to acquire it. In addition, avoidance of foods is a special form of long-term memory. We come prepared to associate gustatory information with visceral distress. This is an ancient system that underlies a specific adaptation – memory and learning about food sources (Garcia et al., 1974; Rozin, 1976).

ENVIRONMENTAL SALIENCE, MEMORY, CORTISOL, AND THE BRAIN. Many different neuronal systems underlie the conversion of reverberating circuits into memory; natural and experimental interference has long been known to compromise the consolidation of the encoding process that produces memory (Erickson, Mah, Schulkin, Charney, & Drevets, 2005; Lupien & McEwen, 1997; McGaugh, 2000, 2003). Many of us remember the death of John F. Kennedy when we were schoolchildren; we knew it was an important event. In this context, cortisol helps solidify the memory as the memory is encoded in our brains. But deep trauma and high levels of cortisol for long periods degrade memory, and degrade a consolidation process for the storage of memory in cephalic systems (Erickson et al., 2005; Lupien, Maheu, Tu, Fiocco, & Schramek, 2007). The amygdala, hippocampus, and caudate nucleus within the basal ganglia are important for the consolidation process (McGaugh, 2003) (see Figure 3.5).

Thus, hormones such as cortisol can either facilitate or degrade memory consolidation, depending on the length of time and degree to which they are activated (McGaugh, 2003). Adrenal steroid activation can induce diverse regulation of chemical signals that underlie salience (Berridge, 2007; Berridge & Robinson, 1998; Dallman, 2007) and attentiveness to environmental events. In both animal and human studies, infusions of cortisol immediately after an event can facilitate the memory. The basal lateral region of the amygdala and the projections to and from cortical and subcortical sites are critical for the facilitation of many forms of memory (McGaugh, 2003; Roozendaal, 2000; Aggleton, 2000).

The amygdala is, in part, like a big megaphone broadcasting the significance of an event to other brain regions. The other regions then encode the formation of memory. Thus the wake-up hormone, cortisol, facilitates diverse kinds of memories and memory storage via noradrenergic activation of the basal lateral amygdala, which then broadcasts the information to different brain regions (McGaugh, 2003; Roozendaal, 2000). Glucocorticoid hormones activate the amygdala and increase attention to diverse objects, including facial expressions (Erickson et al., 2005).

Cortisol can also influence the performance of declarative memory tasks and tasks of memory for emotional information. The cognitive effects of exogenous glucocorticoids depend on the dose and time period between administration and testing, as well as on the time of testing within the diurnal pattern of cortisol secretion (Lupien et al., 2007; Lupien & McEwen, 1997; Erickson, Drevets, & Schulkin, 2003).

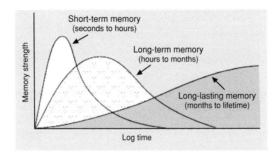

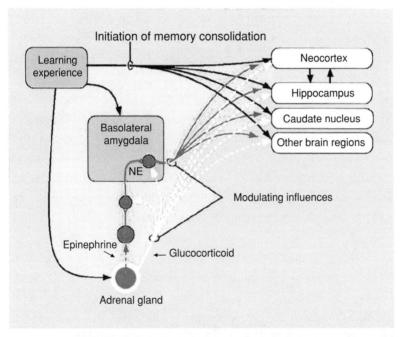

FIGURE 3.5. Schematic of the consolidation process and how glucocorticoids and epinephrine can modulate memory consolidation processes via the amygdala. A learning experience activates brain processes in numerous brain regions. It will also activate glucocorticoid secretion that can influence peripheral arousal mechanisms, such as epinephrine, and numerous brain regions. The basal lateral complex of the amygdala plays a central role by being modulated by glucocorticoids and, in turn, memory consolidation processes in other brain regions. Norepinephrine modulation of amygdala function is illustrated, but other neurotransmitter systems, like dopamine, serotonin, and acetylcholine, also influence the amygdala (adapted from McGaugh, 2000).

Cortisol facilitates attentional states, increases incentive salience, increases arousal, and enhances attention to sensory stimuli. It may also enhance activity in the basal lateral area of the amygdala through its effects on norepinephrine, thereby consolidating memory, especially memory for emotional stimuli or autobiographical events (Erickson et al., 2003, 2005). Autobiographical memories are tied to episodic memory, which refers to memory of specific events occurring in an individual. This link suggests that increased levels of cortisol may enhance memory during emotionally arousing events (McGaugh, 2000, 2003) and facilitate or degrade (depending on the level of cortisol) the storage of autobiographical memories (Erickson et al., 2005) (see Figure 3.6).

What evolved in humans is the luxury to think about time, in terms of both personal and historical events. This ability to conceptualize is an important part of humans as a species. Diverse cognitive machinations contribute to declarative and procedural, episodic and cultural, semantic, and short- and long-term memory (Baddley et al., 2002). These are the kinds of mechanisms, along with the basic clock mechanisms, that underlie our historical sensibility.

EXPANDING MEMORY: THE BEGINNING OF HISTORY. As we have seen, a major feature of our cognitive arsenal is the broad array of memory systems, both internal and external. The external features blend effortlessly into the cognitive features within us (Clark, 1997, 2003). Humans are endlessly bootstrapping external objects to hold onto memory. Some features of internal memory, what Karl Lashley (1951) called the "endgram," and external memory, what Merlin Donald (1991) called the "exogram," are depicted in Table 3.2.

We unload memory storage onto our surroundings and into the spaces we inhabit (Clark, 1997, 1999). As we decrease the cognitive load, we make familiar what is around us. The exogram is a metaphor for this. It is an important adaptation that, after learning something, we can externalize it and make it part of the everyday. An exogram is

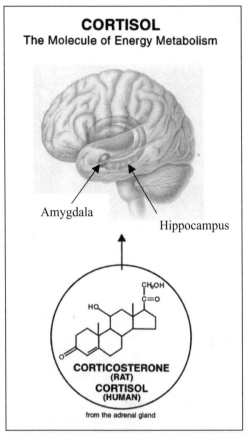

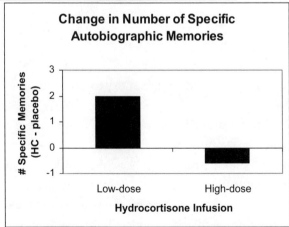

FIGURE 3.6. Effect of adrenal steroid (cortisol) on autobiographical memory (Erickson et al., 2003).

TABLE 3.2. *Properties of internal and external memory compared*

Internal memory record (endgram)	External memory record (exogram)
Fixed physiological media	Virtually unlimited physical media
Constrained format, depending on type of record, and cannot be reformatted	Unconstrained format, may be reformatted
Impermanent and easily distorted	May be made much more permanent
Large but limited capacity	Overall capacity unlimited
Limited size of single entries (e.g., names, words, images, narratives)	Single entries may be very large (e.g., novels, encyclopedic reports; legal systems)
Retrieval paths constrained; main cues for recall are proximity, similarity, and meaning	Retrieval paths unconstrained; any feature or attribute of the items can be used for recall
Limited perceptual access in audition, virtually none in vision	Unlimited perceptual access, especially in vision
Organization is determined by the modality and manner of initial experience	Spatial structure and temporal juxtaposition may be used as an organizational device
The working area of memory is restricted to a few innate systems (e.g., speaking or subvocalizing to oneself, visual imagination)	The working area of memory is an external display that can be organized in a rich, three-dimensional spatial environment
Literal retrieval from internal memory achieved with weak activation of perceptual brain areas; precise and literal recall is rare, often misleading	Retrieval from external memory produces full activation of perceptual brain areas; external activation of memory can appear to be clearer and more intense than reality

Source: Donald, 1991.

continuous with the world, and memory too is continuous with the external world.

One adaptive feature in our evolution is the extent to which, after we learn something, we create props in the environment to activate systems for performance (e.g., recognition of an event, a person, or how to do something). Memory is thus not strictly in our heads. The exograms are perhaps more apparent to us daily and are thus continuous with endogenous cognitive systems (Clark, 1997; Donald, 2004; Wheeler, 2005). At times it appears as unclear where the endgram ends and the exogram begins. Our cognitive world is rich with exograms that serve to guide behavior and that are continuous with endogenous cognitive mechanisms.

Monuments, de facto examples of exograms, hold one forcefully to the past. Walking amid pillars of antiquity, such as the Colosseum in Rome, one marvels at the splendor of the society that produced it, which rings loud among the statuesque stance of its fallen past. That history in turn is somewhat incorporated into the culture that superseded it – Christianity – or the Renaissance resurgence of the glories of antiquity (Burckhardt, 1929/1958). The remembered past liberates, as its ornaments bespeak an archaeological articulation of the past. Perhaps the repressive Scholastic beliefs of the medieval age gave rise to the urge to move back historically and to regather the ancients. With the pillars of an ancient aesthetic and texts to serve as vehicles of knowledge, the move into the Renaissance was made possible.

HISTORICAL INQUIRY: HUMANS EMBODIED IN THEIR PAST AND NARRATIVES ABOUT US. Historical sensibility is more than just the mnemonic abilities humans share with other animals. Even the simplest of animals can remember events from their pasts. To have a sense of history is to move toward the point at which culture begins. Primary memory mechanisms are the underpinning of historical sensibility (e.g., Bergson, 1908/1991). As memory turns to history, nature converges with culture.

History is as old as humanity; when humans started to tell one another about events from their childhoods, to construct mythologies, or to recount hunting trips, they started to narrate history. The narratives people tell are the vehicles of agency revealed to others over time. History reveals the varied expressions of human experience (Vico, 1744/1970; Butterfield, 1981) – the diverse beliefs and desires that have been expressed over time by individuals and their cultures. Experience is often ephemeral; it is lost without a trace if left to itself. At its best, history intervenes to preserve culture and to imbue wisdom.

Our sense of time is rooted in our sense of space; life history is about a trajectory of movement through space. One such conception adapted from the work of Mark Johnson (1993) is depicted here:

Movement

↓

Purposive action

↓

Longer-term purposive activity

↓

Living a life

In historical narrative, one gives an account of how something occurred and then vanished with little or nothing extant. History is therefore a person's or a culture's testimony of what happened and what was accomplished. Journeys' metaphors (Johnson, 1993, 2007), and metaphorical reasoning are important parts of our cognitive architecture (Fauconnier & Turner, 2003; Lakoff & Johnson, 1999; Pinker, 2007). History matters: not just to preserve but to perceive anew, to reexperience and to take account of what happened. To experience the past – to learn from it, appreciate it, and understand it – we need the diverse expressions of historical narratives (Dilthey, 1926/1961; Nash, 1967).

History is the way in which we come to terms with the past and learn from it. But there are many instances of rewriting the past and making it fit our wishes (e.g. Medvedev, 1989; Vico, 1744/1970; Finley, 1971; Galison, 1999; Israel, 2001; Koyre, 1961; Kuhn 1962/1971; Machiavelli, 1525/1988. Interpretation of our surroundings – the basic stuff of history making – pervades this sense of our existence. For example, contemporary Japanese textbooks omit accounts of atrocities committed by the Japanese against the Chinese both before and during World War II. When a culture insulates itself in this manner and lacks a historical record of integrity as it faces the past, barbaric behavior can resurface. The rationalization and glorification of deadly wrongs can glamorize and justify any kind of ghastly act. After all, the Nazis wrote their destiny in the face of the fallen Weimar Republic. Thus, there is the ever-alluring fantasy of the past: that mythical homecoming for things long gone and the secret urge to return to the secure, the safe, and the stable. Rambling within one's memory can evoke tremendous nostalgia. To retell the dreams that once seemed real is a powerful force. So our stories glow and grow – the real blurred into the fanciful, the fanciful glimmering with purported truth. History in this light is a deceptive and seductive pull backward; it is devolution not evolution. It is a sign of not being able to look forward or to plan ahead; it is a sign of immaturity. History told as nostalgia is childlike. In the hands of despots, historical narrative is dangerous and damning. Past events glorified by nostalgia can lead to sentimental amnesia.

When history is masked as a nostalgic longing, it blurs our recollections into sentiments that bind and blind. As part of our history in America, we relive the paradox of exaggerated liberty on the one hand and chattel slavery on the other. Native Americans were systematically driven from their homes in enormous numbers, yet a groundwork was laid that fermented a great culture filled with optimism and the promise of change through unfettered entrepreneurial activities (Menand, 2001). We look into the past to broaden our scope and to bear responsibility for the historical record (Woodward, 1955/1966).

History is also, potentially, a vehicle to reach out to others, because reconciliation is at the heart of coming to terms with the past – the good and the bad. To remain bitter and defeated is to surrender to the past. To be sure, sometimes the weight of the past is just that heavy. However, the challenge is to use the past, to know it without being consumed by it. Historical knowledge is our tie to the past, but it need not and should not be a binding rope; the objective is not to rewrite history or to self-flagellate but to use history as the lens of self-understanding in a sense of self-corrective inquiry (Foner, 2002).

At its best, historical narrative is tied to the re-creation of experience (Collingwood, 1946/1956, 1929/1978). By reconstructing and interpreting the meaning of the past (Berlin, 1976, 1991), historians can re-create the past, not as a dead monument but as a sign of lived experience. Historical hypotheses can inform present experience by rendering the past alive, with its contingencies, the use of tools, and the means of interpretation. History is about change and becoming (Croce, 1941), about particulars and contingency (Rickert, 1929/1986), and about coming to terms with the past (see Figure 3.7).

History is also replete with our sense of agency, of human beings struggling to persevere on trajectories abounding with human meaning and a fragile, evolving humanity. Humans are prone to construct stories about our past, about who we are. It is a core feature of us. Historical sensibility matters for capturing something of existence, of being embodied in action, of being present. The issue is capturing history without historicism, with minimal distortion. Self-corrective inquiry needs to be presented, cultivated, and knotted to historical reconstruction. Self-corrective inquiry starts early in development (Dewey, 1938; Kagan, 1984; Meltzoff, 2004). Children are not little investigators, but obviously we come prepared early to begin investigative events, to discern discrepancies, and to search for coherence. Historical sensibility needs to be anchored to this natural propensity.

The myth that knowledge always liberates is just that – a myth. The Baconian call for truth, with the idea that liberty and progress are the vectors of historical events, is mistaken. Although trends of progress can be discerned in some turns of history, those trends are discontinuous, abrupt, and at times disheartening. History has no built-in necessity toward that end.

Although history shows no linear trend, perhaps there are cycles in history, ups and downs of better and worse, human expressions analogous to economic trends (Elster, 1983/1988; Schumpeter, 1934).

FIGURE 3.7. Vietnam Memorial, Washington, D.C. (Yansen & Schulkin, 2007).

There seem, however, to be no discernible historical laws governing the rise and fall of nations, despite assertions of the cyclic flow of historical events. As in the life of an individual, there are good times and bad, some of which one causes and others due to calamities beyond one's control. Indeed, slovenly forms of expression contributed to the downfall of the Romans as much as did the rise of rival powers and the shortsightedness of the Roman vision. The cyclic rise and fall of nations thus reveals no godlike plan of parallel theological movement.

Perhaps history reveals a non-Darwinian form of evolution. The desire for security and safety is a key feature of animal adaptation, but so too is curiosity and expansiveness, and all of these vary among species. The basic human need for a haven of safety amid times of genocide was a cumulative need, as the desires of one generation contributed to the actions of the next. But what might be a good idea in this case – to mobilize a people – can expire within a few generations.

Jean-Baptiste Lamarck (1809/1984) captured the spirit of biology, which is striving (see Burkhardt, 1977/1995). Although Lamarckian concepts have found little justification in biological evolution, they have relevance to social evolution. The striving for social justice for women and minorities in this country are but two examples. Historical sensibility is the lifeblood of our cultural legacy (Woodward, 1986, 1989). An important component of this legacy is the autobiographical accounts of how individuals experience the world. We learn from inquiring into how and why people do what they do and how they experience the world. This is equally true for the laboratory scientist, the field biologist, and the molecular biologist. Inquiry is one of the ways that humans come to terms with what we do. It is the way we come to appreciate others. Underlying this orientation to historical inquiry is an early predilection to detect the sense of agency in others, their desires and beliefs, and to understand agents as animate.

CONCLUSION. Human beings reveal diverse forms of cognitive systems, one of which is our capacity for memory (e.g., Rozin, 1976; Schacter, 1996; Tulving, 2002). Hormones such as cortisol, by facilitating neuronal expression, can enhance or degrade memory (McGaugh, 2003). Diverse kinds of memory systems contribute to the construction of history. There is no one part of the brain for history per se, but rather many kinds of memory systems that contribute to our historical sensibility. The memory systems are not in isolation; they are continuous with the larger cultural world that we inhabit, and with internal timing mechanisms, such as daily, monthly, and yearly clocks, that, along with our many memory systems, set the neural and cognitive conditions for historical sensibility. Historical sensibility is fundamentally linked to our sense of agency, of understanding others, and of gaining a perspective on ourselves and our position in the world (Collingwood, 1946/1956).

Something unique emerged in us through evolution. Greater motor and cognitive flexibility resulted in the use of our cognitive arsenal with the onset of memory systems external to us. The expansion of symbols culminated in theoretical speculations (Donald, 1991, 2004). The onset of culture expanded memory beyond our internal machinations. But importantly, from the onset, memory has been anchored to our sense of objects, the adaptive systems that tie us to the discernment of events, our sense of action and embodied existence (Gibbs, 2006; Glenberg, 1997). Context pervades memory fields (Clark, 1999; Gibson, 1966; Glenberg, 1997). Time "travel" is an important ingredient in our cognitive ascent (Suddenhorf & Corballis, 1997, 2007) and a part of understanding our personal trajectories.

Our evolved brain has the ability for both destructive and constructive behavior. A bigger brain does not make us wiser, but in our case (unlike that of the cow), it just means smarter. Our evolutionary ascent is, after all, pregnant with the legacy of our historical blunders (Dewey, 1925/1989; Walton, 2002). The evolution that Dewey understood was a progressive form of evolution. For him, human ingenuity and self-correction were to be harnessed toward worthy human ends, enriched by an understanding of human history while couched in a psychobiological perspective (Pauly, 1987; Weidman, 1999). Progress, the deepening of human experience through an appreciation of one another, is something humans can achieve through the creative use of our problem-solving abilities. But this lofty desire competes with many other motives, perhaps ones that are more powerful and established.

As we evolved, we accrued knowledge in a biological context. Increased problem-solving abilities, along with social bonding, allowed us to become empathic machines. We further expanded our abilities because of technological innovations, such as when, with the use of telescopes, we effectively became able to lengthen our eyesight. Our sensory systems were expanded by our desires and passed on by our culture. Nature and culture are different concepts, not because in some way they are not constructions but because the impact of Darwinian evolution is felt in one and the impact of Lamarckian evolution is felt in the other. Of course, concepts of culture are also battling with one another, dying out, and being superseded or discarded. We destroy and rebuild, endlessly. As a result, historical sensibility, when demythologized, must be knotted to self-awareness (e.g. Woodward, 1986, 1989).

One should also be aware of discontinuity (Dupré, 1993) and of continuity where it manifests itself. Moreover, it is an aberration of inquiry to assert that knowledge is only power, and that power is the only significant fact of discourse (Derrida, 1972/1981). Tying this propensity of historical sensibility to self-corrective inquiry is a normative goal. Linking diverse cognitive systems that reflect flexibility, adaptive goals, and the rich use of symbols to self-awareness is an achievement of our species (Mithen, 1996; Rozin, 1976).

This is the material for embodied cognition – the experience of history, memory systems rich in lexical content and autobiographical material. Any form of human cognitive explanation reeks with human interests, concerns, and desires; objectivity is not neutral, whether historical or otherwise (Haskell, 1998). An expanded sense of agency linked to others, locked to a form of perception of others being alive, is a running theme.

When cultural memory is fragmented and disjointed and only meager attempts are made to integrate it, historical consciousness quickly fades into fatigued nostalgia (Lewis, 2004). Conversely, the dangerous potential of the mass media to overdramatize the present beyond its worth, coupled with an exaggerated narcissism, warps the historical scope that is essential for depth of understanding. From a positive standpoint, the storytelling spirit of learning from the past, together with an ardent and inquiring spirit, are essential for historical understanding and for coming to terms with the past (Collingwood, 1946/1956; Vico, 1744/1970; Butterfield, 1981; Berlin, 1976, 1991).

We are a species that takes responsibility, historically emboldened by clock and memory mechanisms that we have expanded to symbolic horizons. The imperative normative goal is not to trample on others – but to respect the agency of others, their beliefs and desires. Historical sensibility, humbled by the abuse of monolithic mythologies, is a small protective factor. Self-reflective and self-corrective inquiry ought to be humbling. The sense of power that we have achieved should render us modest, thoughtful, and kind, but like all things it is frail. Our condition is social, historical, and contextual. These virtues are easily trampled upon, as are all the truly good things about the human condition.

4

Educational Sensibilities

An education which does not begin by evoking initiative and end by encouraging it must be wrong. For its whole aim is the production of active wisdom.
– Alfred North Whitehead, *Aims of Education*

To accept and, ultimately, understand evolving conceptions of ourselves and our human past, present, and uncertain future, we need to be educated. No one blueprint should or need be proposed, except that, at the heart, there should be some sense of being experimental, self-corrective, and kind to others. Reason needs to be demythologized and placed in instrumental and incremental units (e.g., Simon, 1962, 1982).

Underlying all forms of learning are cognitive events that set the proper conditions for learning, along with a propensity for self-correction. An experimental spirit is a humbling affair; we are wrong a fair amount of the time, and we should be aware of that. Also, hypotheses are shared – they are tentative.

Our brains are prepared to understand and consider the experiences of others through prosocial dispositions, which set the stage for appreciating others (Darwin 1859/1958, 1871/1874, 1872/1965) and facilitate social skills. We are drawn to tell our autobiographies and give away what we have learned, what we know; the human narrative is a fundamental way in which we learn from and about one another. Narrative tales convey a sense of other people's experience. When this consideration is linked to self-corrective learning and inquiry, our

94

horizons can be broadened; after all, that is why open-mindedness is a virtue. Neurogenesis, a phenomenon that exemplifies lifelong learning, is both a metaphor and a reality for lifetime inquiry and rejuvenation. The evolved cortical and subcortical mantle, neural capacity for neural genesis, and an abundant amount of neural tissue underlie this capacity.

This chapter conveys the historical trends of what seems important for the process of developing educational sensibilities in the Western sense, beginning with the classical period and culminating in the present. Underlying the historical development of the educational process always are the base notes of learning from others, from their experiences.

KNOWING OTHERS: ONE FORM OF TEACHING AND CULTURAL LEARN-ING. Learning is indeed an innate proclivity (Marler, 2000), with the stage set by a group of basic cognitive preconditions. The cognitive revolution in biology in the 1970s unleashed an appreciation of the diverse cognitive systems that underlie education and learning (Gardner, 1985). Education may be viewed in part as releasing cognitive abilities, finding outlets, and deepening the richness of basic cognitive hardware (Carey, 2004). The student learns to carry out and design experiments, to develop theories, and to conduct various levels of analysis. Theory building and the link to evidence is at the heart of inquiry and should also be at the heart of education (e.g., Carey & Smith, 1993; Dewey, 1938/1972).

Although young children are not little scientists, humans come prepared to hypothesize and test to forge a sense of stability, predictability, and coherence. The knowing process is tied, as I have indicated, to the gymnasium as Dewey suggested (1909/1975, 1938/1972); but it is a social gymnasium in the larger social world in which we have to understand and adapt. Knowledge is in part a contact sport, social in nature, tied to others, and emboldened by body sensibility and imagination (Johnson, 1987/1990; Schulkin, 2004).

Metaphor plays an essential role in our ability to understand the world we are inhabiting and in trying to understand others (e.g., Falconnier & Turner, 2003; Lakoff & Johnson, 1999). Metaphoric extension and expansion of one set of events to another is an important cognitive mechanism in coming to understand others and what they are trying to achieve, to learn from them and ascertain what we are striving for; metaphoric expression pervades our cognitive capabilities as well as our scientific lexicon (e.g., mirror neurons).

What is emboldened in us is an innate ability tied to successful, broad-based problem solving through, in part, the simulation of events, which captures the human experiences that inform and facilitate learning (Carey & Gelman, 1991; Carey & Smith, 1993; Gopnik & Meltzoff, 1997; Keil, 1983, 2007; Meltzoff, 2004).Education is a continuation of this ability to probe and test, and self-corrective inquiry may be viewed as essential to education; inquiry is, in part, a conception of an educational laboratory (Dewey, 1902/1974).

The laboratory metaphor conveys the sense that inquiry is lifelong and that our ideas need to be tested. Self-corrective inquiry is at the heart of knowledge, science, and understanding; it bootstraps off the cognitive hardware (Carey, 2004) and the helpful aids in the environment we create and to which we adapt (Clark, 1997, 1999; Donald, 1991, 2004; Glenberg, 1997; Glenberg & Kaschak, 2002).

At the heart of learning is something social: learning from other people's experiences. The cognitive orientation of our species and related primates is social (Dunbar, 2003; Humphrey, 1976). Young children go from making broad imitative representations to discerning and using to their own advantage the beliefs and desires of others in orchestrating behavioral responses (Tomasello & Call, 1997; Tomasello, Carpenter, Call, Behne, & Moll, 2004; see Table 4.1).

What is distinctive about us, though our species is not entirely alone in this (Melis, Hare, & Tomasello, 2006), is the degree to which we share and participate toward common ends; shared intentions linked to the considerations of others is one of our most important

TABLE 4.1. *Major steps in human cognitive development, with specific focus on social-cultural dimensions and their effects*

Infancy: Understanding others as intentional
  1. Following attention and behavior of others: social referencing, attention following, imitating acts on objects
  2. Directing attention and behavior of others: imperative gestures, declarative gestures
  3. Symbolic play with objects: playing with "intentionality" of object
Early childhood: Language
  1. Linguistic symbols and predication: intersubjective representations
  2. Event categories: events and participants in one schema
  3. Narratives: Series of interrelated events with some constant participants
Childhood: Multiple perspectives and representational redescriptions
  1. Theory of mind: seeing situation both as it is and as other believes it to be
  2. Concrete operations: seeing events or object in two ways simultaneously
  3. Representational redescription: seeing own behavior/cognition from outside perspective

Source: Tomasello & Call, 1997.

cognitive mechanisms (Baron-Cohen, 1995, 2000; Tomasello, Savage-Rumbaugh, & Kruger, 1993; Tomasello et al., 2004). Children express the rudiments of this ability before two years of age (Kagan, 1984; Wellman, 1990; Bartsch & Wellman, 1995). Shared space (see, e.g., Mead, 1932/1980, 1934/1972) is bound to shared representations of others – of their experiences, beliefs, desires, and goals. Several factors are critical: the recognition of animation; awareness of the goals and pursuits of other individuals; and the recognition of their beliefs, desires, future plans (Tomasello et al., 1993). Each of these cognitive events is critical for our cultural evolution. They rewire something often called dialogic inquiry (Tomasello & Call, 1997; Wells, 1999), which is a shared sense of inquiry (Peirce, 1899/1992).

Our intentions link us to others; our recognition of others' intentions and our shared intentions provide the common currency of shared experiences (e.g., Schutz, 1932/1967; Frith & Wolpert, 2003). Shared experience and its recognition are important parts of our social understanding of one another, giving us shared meanings, shared intentions, and recognition of others (e.g., Fromm, 1947; Goffman,

1971; Grice, 1957; Sabini & Schulkin, 1994). The pervasive sense of others is an early adaptation, a piece of our survival.

It is not surprising, given that we are primarily visual animals, that eye contact is pivotal for getting a window into others (Adolphs, 1999; Baron-Cohen et al., 2000), and that gaze following might be linked to primate evolution (Barth et al., 2007; Emery, Lorincz, Perrett, Oram, & Baker, 1997), in addition to the expansion of cortical tissue (Barton, 2006). Figure 4.1 depicts one anatomical view of visual input with regard to social milieu. Visual information is the quickest way we share intentions and experiences (see Figure 4.1).

Shared intentions are the lifeblood of human meaning and human connectedness (Jaspers, 1913/1997). We share our life stories, our life trajectories, our sense of place and time, of being connected to others, the pain, the perseverance and frailty, the reprieves and exuberance, the mundane and beautiful. There is nothing abstract about this. It is indeed an important cognitive adaptation, a fundamental way in which we also share vulnerabilities (Nussbaum, 2004).

Many forms of perception, including joint attention to tasks and objects, demonstrate how early this appears. As Tomasello et al. (2004) recognized, the key feature in collaborative endeavors is the ability to share intentions, to recognize agency amid animacy. Before two years of age, these cognitive abilities are pervasive. The social act (Mead, 1932/1980, 1934/1972) – my consideration of you and your consideration of me (whether good or bad) – is an intersubjective event. Learning from others is embodied in the engagement of others. Collaborative endeavors are not an aberration but an essential feature of our species, and problem solving is often knotted to others, particularly through education. Classical pragmatism emphasized this sort of shared sense of problem solving (see Smith, 1970, 1985).

HISTORICAL CONTEXTS. The classical worlds of Greece and Rome emphasized rhetoric, mathematics, music, and muscle. To participate in the polity meant to speak well and persuasively. To be skilled in

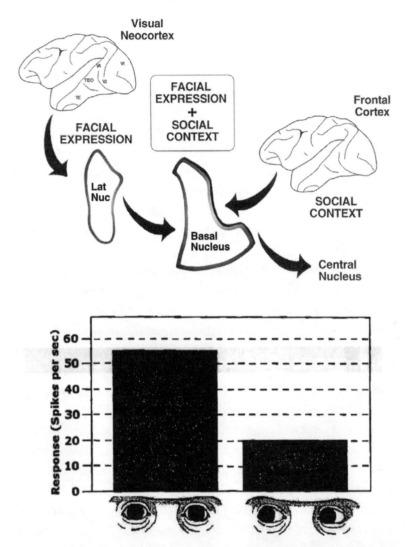

FIGURE 4.1. The hypothesis of amygdala function in primate social cognition suggests that social stimuli, such as facial expressions, enter the lateral nucleus of the amygdala from visual neocortex. Facial expressions are usually communicated within a particular social context (e.g., during an aggressive encounter by a particular individual). The basal nucleus receives a projection from the lateral nucleus (expressions) and projections from the orbitofrontal cortex. Information concerning social context (based on stored social knowledge of group members) is conveyed to the basal nucleus from the orbitofrontal cortex, where an appropriate response is then initiated via basal nuclei projections back to the neocortex and via central nucleus projections to effector structures, such as the brain stem and hypothalamus (Emery & Amaral, 2000). Neurophysiological responses (bottom) from cells in the superior temporal sulcus of the macaque to indirect and direct eye contact of conspecifics (adapted from Perrett & Mistlin, 1990).

rhetoric, the art of defended speech, was imperative, and the way to engage the public was to reach them through speech (e.g., Brehier, 1931/1965).

To think rigorously, however, required the use of form. For the Greeks, mathematics served this purpose. They believed that mathematical knowledge was innately given, citing as evidence slaves who had never been exposed to any geometry but who demonstrated mathematical competence when questioned skillfully. Education triggered and made manifest this inborn competence while instilling a discipline for thought.

Without harmony, the Greeks thought, discipline would be compulsive and hard, the rhetoric short and stumpy. The world could be interpreted in harmonies, in natural rhythms, and one could learn to muse through harmonic, playful rhetoric that was rigorously formed.

An educated person of the classical Greek period was expected to speak well, to reason rigorously, and to experience the muses through harmonics. Muscle or physical prowess was equally part of the mind's development; classical philosophers saw mind and body as united because they exposed the world. An educated person was a mind at ease orchestrating a body (see Figure 4.2). The educated person who spoke in well-formed verse with physical prowess had presence and participated in the polity.

During the medieval period in Western society, an educated person was well acquainted with architectonics. In this period, argument had reached a zenith as the measure of truth; this was the age of argument, ornament, and cathedrals – dialect in stone (see Haskins, 1923/1957). Rhetoric, now masterfully pursued, was embedded in elaborate dialect. Physical prowess was valued but as a worldly virtue; authority predominated. One's identity as an educated person was in deciphering the arguments, the forms of expression, the legislative authority – the grand cathedrals.

The educated person embodied a different form at the end of the Middle Ages, at the dawn of the age of humanism. This was the

FIGURE 4.2. Expression of different disciplines.

beginning of the elevation of the individual (Barzun, 1989). Argument by itself was inadequate. Authority alone was not sufficient. Now, discovery through explanation of the world predominated. Experimentation, innovation, and individual expression constituted the paradigm toward which the educated person strove. A rediscovery of classical writings refueled the quest to explore and inquire. Dogma was challenged. Nothing was simply given – including elaborate argument, no matter how well formed and architectonic. The human spirit had become center stage for the educated person. Knowledge of the world required individual acts of human expression.

Although empiricism, rather than rationalism, began to dominate, what was valued even more was a sense of creativity, wonder, and exploration. It was deemed more important to discover knowledge than merely to argue for it. The educated person was a master of exploration, whose method was to test, to hypothesize, and to predict, and whose expression was radical and individual. The Renaissance person was also well rounded (Burckhardt, 1929/1958).

Humanistic thought laid the groundwork for the development of modern modes of inquiry in the seventeenth and eighteenth centuries; a romantic sensibility pervaded an educated acumen in which nature was alive (Clark, 2006; Collingwood, 1945/1976, 2001). Modern inquiry now took shape. To be educated still meant to be steeped in the classics and skilled in the use of elaborate, architectonic argument. Experimentation and mathematics, however, rather than rhetoric, were considered the two roads to truth. The educated person was versed in all these skills and knowledge. The educated person adopted either rationalism or empiricism according to language and culture, though, of course, each of these cultures mixed the two because argument and experiment are intimately connected.

The early-modern world saw the emergence of a new and vitally important factor for the educated: reason by probability, in addition to logic, mathematics, and rhetoric. Probabilistic reasoning was the new way of making a case in courts of law, the math of jurisprudence for those who argued a legal case (Hacking, 1975, 1990, 1999). The advent of probabilistic reasoning augured the breakdown of certainty as the measure of truth. This turn of events was ironic, because of its coincidence with revitalization of mathematical reasoning and its style. The educated person was schooled in rational deduction, mathematics, logical induction, probability, and rhetoric. Nature was now more than ever investigated by using the wit of invention and the flair of hypothesis, the tools of the educated person. When making a case, depending on the subject matter, one used all forms of reasoning. Rhetoric was still the flower of thought, residing somewhere amid mathematics, science, and philosophy.

Although Reformation theology stressed the importance of personal interpretation of the Bible and thus ushered in a world in which many more people could read, only the aristocracy could truly afford the luxury of a full education (Koyre, 1961). In public life, the educated person was a cultivated individual possessed of good taste and manners and displaying proper proportionality. Being educated required knowledge of culture and history, languages, the human and social sciences (anthropology), the natural sciences, and mathematics. Measured and cultivated responses, moreover, necessitated a working knowledge of other cultures and languages. To be proficient in the science of human nature was therefore a necessity in one's negotiations with others.

Knowledge of mathematics, and an understanding of technology and the mechanisms of physical interactions, was considered necessary to foster economic productivity and growth. As an educated person, the aristocrat was truly worldly in outlook, possessing an international perspective that reached beyond national borders to a world history, a working vocabulary of the biological sciences, and an understanding of the new symbolic logic.

Semiotics, the study of signs and their meanings, was an essential component of this education (e.g., Peirce, 1899/1992; Smith, 1970, 1985). Meanings were to be discerned, as hermeneutics replaced rhetoric and the art of interpretation was tied to understanding the world and one's place in it. The educated person needed to be able to speak the various interpretations of the world – the theological, the physical, the biological, and the psychological. The cultivated intellect, the aristocratic scholar, could engage a variety of interpretations on the world and was comfortable in the parlor of thought.

With the rise of public education in the modern age, an extended education was afforded to many more people, not just the aristocratic few. It is one of our central goods – universal primary education. As education has become public and more accessible to ordinary people, we have increasingly emphasized problem solving. John Dewey's educational philosophy (1916, 1920/1948, 1938/1979), which still enjoys wide popularity and influence in the United States, is good evidence of this. The perceived goal of education has shifted to confronting problems and invoking solutions. The educated person has become a problem solver, culling from mathematics, the sciences, language, and art. In the modern age, the educated person engages matters in an experimental fashion, with an appreciation of hypotheses and the creative genesis of ideas.

PRAGMATISM: EDUCATIONAL ORIENTATION THAT EMPHASIZES IN-QUIRY AND HYPOTHESIS TESTING. It is fundamental to the pragmatist's notion of inquiry, whether in history, art, science, or mathematics, that the hypothetical feature of all forms of inquiry is prominent. What is important is a large sense of experimentation. Some hypotheses solve problems and are our tools for understanding the dilemmas of life.

Ideally, the experimentalist embodies the pursuit of ideas, but without a sense of history, no context for understanding could exist. The history of ideas is the history of trying to understand ourselves, our sense of agency with what is around us, and where we are or should be going, replete with an appreciation of what Whitehead (1933/1961) termed "The Adventures of Ideas."

The tools used to seek this understanding are as broad and diverse as the problem. Tool use is therefore no longer considered an inferior activity. Common knowledge, like common faith, is no longer aristocratic (see Figure 4.3). Labor is at the heart of education, and the sweat of the experimentalists is the perfume of the inquirer. Theory and practice are no longer separate.

As tool users and problem solvers, artisans tied theory to practice, and their achievement was to tie the mind to the body; cognitive resources innervated bodily ability (Anderson, 1997; Clark, 1983; Franklin, 1726, 1757/1987). In the course of history, unfortunately, the educated mind had become too detached from the body (e.g.,

FIGURE 4.3. Benjamin Franklin's Electricity Machine and invention of a fine tool.

classical and modern rationalism, early Christian dualism, or the strictly divorced non-historical perspective of concepts). Only bodies toiled and labored. Only minds had leisure for thought. Thought was pure, whereas the body was brute. Pragmatic educational theory rejects this dichotomy.

Dewey's metaphor of the gymnasium is instructive in this regard. It undercuts the separation of this traditional pernicious bifurcation (see Johnson, 1987/1990; Schulkin, 2004) and replaces it with a sense of cephalic expression across bodily function; the brain reaches into all features of bodily actions; we explore and inhabit a world as bodies, as problem solvers (Merleau-Ponty, 1942/1967). With the realization of problem solving as an exploratory event, the vision for the educated necessarily changed, because problem solving is both an exploratory, intellectual event and a basic biological event that pervades all forms of reasoning (e.g., Casebeer, 2003; Dewey, 1925/1989; Weissman, 2000).

Dewey (1909/1975) emphasized development of character (as did Aristotle), through the development and maintenance of habits of action; many of these habits work to "[bring] the child to realize the social sense of action" (p. 31). Action is rich in moral imagination (Fesmire, 2003; Johnson, 1987/1990); it involves getting oriented toward others, toward the social milieu, toward exploring others and learning how to respond to them and treat them.

The pursuit of inquiry (i.e., learning from the experiences of others), when undertaken with humility, provides a balance among romance, excellence, and generalization (Whitehead, 1929/1958; see also Nussbaum, 1997). Some of us who have pursued academic learning are familiar with the following progression. Our education begins with a mixture of natural curiosity and the seductive pull of a maestro, or professor. He or she commands authority; we follow and become attached. There follows, if we are so fortunate, the romance of the young mind's search for understanding as we discover and explore new vistas of knowledge within an intellectually nurturing environment. The feeling of play that imbues this stage, however, is eventually subsumed within the emergence of labor – not that of the meaningless, rote form but of sustained, focused, and specialized inquiry. Specialization may emerge in each of several topics, such as various areas of science, humanities, and arts. Discipline is required to master the various forms of knowledge; the gymnasium metaphor of Dewey's is, again, an important one to consider.

With discipline now part of the fabric of the person, he or she returns to play, to muse with ideas. The romance with ideas continues, but now theory has given them new meaning, and the infusion of rigorous discipline results in new insights. One of the main ends of the educated person is to help move civilization a bit through understanding, to create innovative technologies for engaging and transforming the world. The educated person is cultivated first by romance, then by rigor and discipline, and then by the expression of ideas.

An experimental demeanor is not only a way of thought but also a way of life. The life of the mind is not sequestered from the world or cloistered from our affairs. To the educated, the call is to bring the mind to the dilemmas of life. Problem solving is at the heart of this endeavor, but it does not make up the whole of it. Reflection and what Peirce (1908/1998) called "musement" are essential for the genesis of ideas. The thinking itself, though disciplined and rigorous, is playful. The educated person plays amid the often harsh and disheartening realities that he or she faces.

WATCHING OTHERS, AGENCY, AND LEARNING. Consider for a moment the modern arena of education at the university level. One of the first things students must know how to do is synthesize, or perhaps disregard, the masses of information with which they are deluged. The modern educated individual is interdisciplinary, conversant in diverse fields of discourse. The mind is trained to move, to be efficient, and yet to muse. The interdependence of all beings on the planet necessitates an interdisciplinary approach to knowledge. Special programs to foster this interdisciplinary approach are required. This is not for everyone but normatively should be a goal. For example, a person-oriented toward environmental/eco-studies is trained in economics, biology, psychology, philosophy, and history. Each discipline is made to bear on the other.

Just as there are critical biological stages in development, there are critical periods for being exposed to educational requirements, particularly in a culture that nominally promotes education (Carey, 2003). It is therefore important for children to be exposed to that which constitutes inquiry: the ability to be interdisciplinary, to engage in discourse in a variety of fields and to connect and differentiate those fields, and to think critically.

A good teacher may convey his or her experiences in science or the humanities, embodied cognition replete with historical trajectory and experiment – how they got to be who they are, and what they think about. The science is at once historical, autobiographical, and factual. It is tied to life, to the drama of pursuing inquiry, of becoming educated. Education is about trying to reach as many young minds as possible, to call them forward and engage them with various media depending on the message and its intended recipient. Students should not be passive; critical thinking is crucial.

Here an apprentice model is called to mind – that is, learning from the experiences of others, capturing a sense of their agency and the trajectory of their journeys in life. The personal bond between a student and a teacher is a vital experience. Teachers offer the promise of the life of education and provide students with a foothold into the world of scholarship. Through this attachment, the student is able to begin his or her journey. The teacher is not just a bearer of facts but represents the life of the educated – what one strives to be. Ideally, students should work closely with their mentors as they are brought into new intellectual worlds. Teachers are then role models for the life of the mind; minds that try to know themselves and their surroundings at many levels of discourse and with a variety of rhetorical expressions. In so doing, the teacher emanates charisma to various degrees. As the teacher's lived experience, with its successes and setbacks, is conveyed to the student, the student is brought into the life of the teacher's mind. Facts are not detached from the body of knowledge but are partially conveyed by the individual quest of the teacher.

This instruction, as conveyed by an individual's experience, is particularly pertinent to interdisciplinary endeavors (Cajal, 1897/1999; Cannon, 1945; Collingwood, 1929/1978). The example of the teacher as an inquirer traversing domains of discourse is instructive in itself. Knowing the teacher is important for the student and helps the student to profit from the teacher's experience. It requires that teachers make themselves vulnerable and expose their own vulnerabilities in discourse with students. As they reveal their own frailties – what and how they have learned, what they know, and what they do not know and would like to know – they draw in students. Through the relaying of individual experience, the acquisition of knowledge is made lively, and the student is engaged. It is, after all, individuals who discover facts, generate theories, and participate in communities. This mode of learning is vital for modern inquiry, for coming to understand other human beings.

Knowledge is, in part, tied to reaching out to and learning from others, and to bringing one another into the community of educated people. This process is particularly important for minorities and the disenfranchised; historically oppressed groups see the dominant group as a foreign body with a voice that speaks differently from their own. Cultivating humanity (see Nussbaum, 1997), or recognizing agents embodied with transparent agency, entails the response to diverse needs without compromising standards of excellence. Whether or not we realize it, we live in cultures within cultures. Cross-fertilization of knowledge between these cultures entails bridging discourse and illuminating our common humanity. One way to do this is to describe one's personal experiences. In the case of the teacher, this description is of the struggle of inquiry. In revealing one's own hurdles, inquiry is demythologized and placed in a human context of shared struggle.

Some purposes of education are to reinforce and open possibilities, to render new horizons to be pursued, and to foster growth and expression. An educator promotes the life of engagement through inquiry. Socratic dialect, coupled with spontaneity, is essential to this endeavor (Neville, 1974; Nussbaum, 1997). Education ought to nurture the growth of wisdom; it is more than teaching derivations, genetic codes, historical episodes, or Shakespearean plots. One cognitive mechanism is coming to understand the beliefs and desires of others and their experiences, which may increase the sense of growing

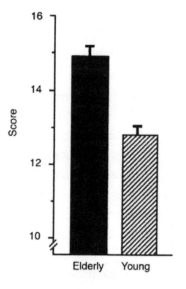

FIGURE 4.4. Elderly individuals are better at theory of mind tasks (Happe et al., 1998).

wiser as one grows older (Happe, Winner, & Bronell, 1998; Schulkin, 2004) (see Figure 4.4).

Learning from others necessitates the unfolding of the lived experiences (Dewey, 1938/1972) of those cumulative moments that have been instructive, that have taught us something that is important for us to know. An educated person has a sense of what matters. At the end of the formal educational process, the student is able to discern when an issue matters and how to reason and inquire further into it by reading, writing, displaying rhetoric, and using other abilities.

The recognition and appreciation of great prose is part of the soul of the educated. Poetry, the mark of the muses, thrives when it is appreciated. The poetic muses enrich and nurture the rhythm of education. Poetry and other forms of artistic expression are essential to the so-called dirty-hands approach to erudition, as is the laboratory, the theater of the educated, extended to the commonplace. Poetry and other art forms are the graceful expressions that mark life as social, sacred, and to be prized. One goal is to cultivate the sacred expressions of our artistic energy. An appreciation of the visual arts, poetry, music, and prose lies at the heart of the educated life (see Nussbaum, 1997; Whitehead, 1933/1961).

An educated person seeks what is interesting, not merely what is true. There cannot be enough humility; knowledge, the recognition of our limitations, is humbling. We are clearly the only species for which pedagogy is lifelong and predominant. One of the ends of education, bound to the social milieu, is the recognition of others (Barzun, 1989). This helps bind us to one another and perhaps fosters the sense that we are after ideas that make a difference. Thus, the use of knowledge is the mark of the educated.

CEPHALIC EXPANSION: LEARNING FROM OTHERS. The components of education throughout history are rooted in brain structure and learning from others. Our brains are prepared to recognize animated objects, motion, and action (Blakemore & Decety, 2001; Wheatley, Milleville, & Martin, 2007). The detection of motion and our sense of being a causal agent are embedded in the concept of agency (e.g., Premack, 1990; Whitehead, 1927/1953). The detection of movement, knotted to intention, is an important discrimination in understanding others (Jacob & Jeannerod, 2003). The brain comes prepared to discern, or at least to try to discern, such relationships.

There exists within us a desire to know and to understand; young children express this desire as they explore the world (Gopnik & Meltzoff, 1997; Kagan, 1984/2002; Meltzoff, 2007). Importantly, cognitive systems for exploration are embedded in sensorimotor explorations (e.g., Smith & Gasser, 2005) (see Figure 4.5). Moreover, one could suggest quite reasonably that the imitative processes seen in neonates with respect to diverse forms of tracking events is an elementary form of learning (Meltzoff & Moore, 1977) made manifest and expanded from following others to engaging others, learning from others, and eventually challenging others, thus generating hypotheses in an expanding, self-corrective process (Gallagher & Meltzoff, 1996; Meltzoff, 2007).

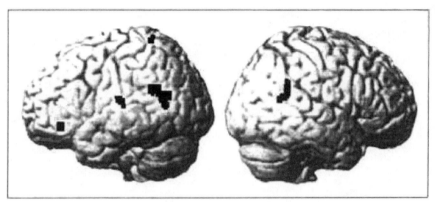

FIGURE 4.5. Looking at and imitating others (following Chaminade et al., 2002; Schulkin, 2000).

This ability to take a perspective is an evolved central state. It is an active state in the consideration of the experiences of others and is tied to communicative competence, essential human bonds (e.g., Decety, 1996; Decety & Jackson, 2006). The information processing that entails this ability is a cognitive and behavioral achievement. Although perception and action are represented in similar regions of the brain (Jeannerod, 1999), these events are linked to broad-based cognitive semantic processing in the organization of action (Nelissen,

Luppino, Vanduffel, Rizzolatti, & Orban, 2005). One precondition for social knowledge is our ability to interpret the behavior of those around us (Baron-Cohen, 1995/2000; Leslie, 1987; Nichols & Stitch, 2003). This has resulted in a prepared ability to link the subject and object in action and to recognize the same as present in others, not only in ourselves.

Such intentional stances are central to problem solving in social interactions. The intentional perspective is anchored to human action and social structure (e.g., Dennett, 1987, 1995). Such social knowledge, discerning the beliefs and desires of others, limits our isolation (Sabini & Schulkin, 1994; Sabini & Silver, 1982). The social milieu includes us as individuals, with the diverse rules that we impose on one another (Bourdieu, 1980/1990; Goffman, 1971; Grice, 1957; Wittgenstein, 1953/1968).

Our sense is focused on others, despite our self-preoccupations. Becoming connected to others involves gaining a foothold into the social world of the moral meaning embodied in everyday common practice. In doing what others do, and in learning from them, we are prepared to learn these things all too easily. Active concern or sympathy for others facilitates social knowledge; it is, in part, a precondition for minimizing bestial expression. Considering the experiences of others makes it more difficult to abuse another person and perhaps increases the sense of conflict in doing so (Greene, Sommerville, Nystrom, Darley, & Cohen, 2001; Moll, de Oliveira-Souza, & Eslinger, 2003; Schulkin, 2004). An elaborate neural circuitry, designed to detect the experiences of others, also discerns their present comfort or noncomfort (Decety & Jackson, 2006; Lamm, Batson, & Decety, 2007).

Notably, results from cognitive neuroscience suggest that imagining the intentional action of another person and actually performing one's own intentional action both engage many of the same underlying information-processing systems in the brain (e.g., Blakemore & Decety, 2001). Motor systems are replete with information-processing

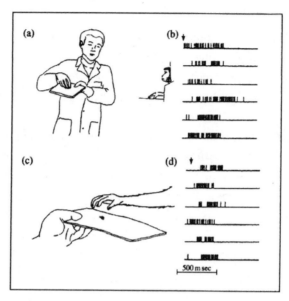

FIGURE 4.6. Mirror neurons in the macaque's prefrontal cortex (di Pellegrino, Fadiga, Fogassi, Gallese, & Rizzolatti, 1992; Jacob & Jeannerod, 2003).

systems in the organization of action (e.g., Jackson & Decety, 2004; Knowlton et al., 1996; Lakoff & Johnson, 1999), and they are also rich in visceral expression (Kelley, 2004; Saper, 1996; Swanson, 2003).

Importantly, imagined activity, in addition to actual interaction with an object, is known to aid learning (Barsalou, 2003; Glenberg, Gutierrez, Levin, Japuntich, & Kaschak, 2004). In general imagined activity, simulated activity generates neuronal populations that would be in use during the actions themselves (Decety, Perani, & Jeannerod, 1994; Hari et al., 1998; Kosslyn, Alpert, & Thompson, 1993). This has become a general rule across a number of both simulated or imagined and real contexts.

Thus, groups of neurons are activated both by performing and by observing intentional action (e.g., Jeannerod, 1999; Nelissen et al., 2005) (see Figure 4.6). One source of evidence is the existence of mirror neurons. Populations of these neurons have been recorded in diverse cortical regions in macaques. Specific neurons fire when the macaque is shown a specific hand movement, and these same neurons also fire when the macaque is performing that movement (e.g., Perrett et al., 1989). In other words, the same regions of the cortex are active both when monkeys observe simple movements and when they perform the same movements.

Similar to these studies in macaques, in human brain-imaging studies, when people were asked to grasp an object or to imagine grasping the same object, regions of the brain linked to movement were activated (Iacoboni et al., 1999). These regions included Brodmann area 6 in the inferior part of the frontal gyrus of both cortical hemispheres, in addition to the anterior cingulate regions and the ventral parietal lobe. Importantly, both the caudate nucleus of the basal ganglia and regions of the cerebellum were also activated. Moreover, a neural system that matches or imitates movement has been shown to include neurons within the left inferior frontal cortex and the caudal region of the right superior parietal lobe – these areas are active when human subjects are asked to observe and imitate finger movements. Watching others is an important source of social information and activates diverse brain regions, in particular dorsal medial prefrontal and medial parietal areas (Iacoboni et al., 2004).

The interesting fact here is that neurons in the brain are active when we do something and when we watch someone else do the same thing. These neurons orchestrate observation and goal-directed action patterns, and perhaps underlie the perception of intentional action. In other words, watching someone perform a behavioral function and performing the same action oneself uses a number of the same brain regions (Iacoboni et al., 1999). That does not mean that they are identical; they are not (Ruby & Decety, 2001). But embedded in these events is the commonsense, justifiable assumption of something shared, of forms of bodily experience, of cognitive systems embedded in sensorimotor experiences (e.g., Lakoff & Johnson, 1999; Merleau-Ponty, 1942, 1967; Prinz, 2004; Schulkin, 2004; Varela, Thompson, & Rosch, 1991; Wilson & Knoblich, 2005). Active concern or sympathy figures in this psychobiological feature of our brains.

Although, again, common areas are activated by perception of agency, such as the superior frontal gyrus, the precentral gyrus, and the occipitotemporal junction (MT/V5) region, regions of the right parietal lobe and somatosensory cortex may be differentially activated with regard to first- and third-person perspective (Ruby & Decety, 2001). Perspective taking may be a feature of gaining access to other people, part of the acculturation process (Baron-Cohen, 1995/2000; Leslie, 1987). It is essential for the development of the concern that we express toward others.

Perhaps the rudiments of this ability to respond to other people's experiences is rooted in the low-level imitative mechanisms and the activation of a number of cortical regions that allow us to learn about others, to get a footing in the world (Decety et al., 1996). A number of brain regions are activated under conditions of similar imitation, such as coming to consider beliefs and desires. They include the superior parietal lobe, inferior parietal lobule, posterior superior temporal sulcus (STS), superior temporal gyrus, and lateral orbital gyrus (Chaminade, Meltzoff, & Decety, 2002). Many of these regions of the brain underlie our social/moral appraisals (Allison, 2001). Thus, various regions of our brains, including the prefrontal, temporal, and parietal cortices, are active when watching others, when imitating their actions, or when doing the actions ourselves (Chaminade et al., 2002; Fogassi et al., 2005; Frith & Frith, 1999; Iacoboni et al., 2004).

SOCIAL CONTACT. As I have indicated throughout the book, within the first few years of life, children have within their cognitive arsenal the ability not only to imitate but also to infer the intentions of others, to recognize safe and dangerous objects, and to detect and protect themselves. Mind is active from the start: an embodied mind in action, in discourse, and in discovery. A large part of the young brain is devoted to discerning the social milieu in which we are adapting, coping, and changing (e.g., Adolphs, 1999; Adolphs & Spezio, 2007; Baron-Cohen, 1995/2000, 2008; Frith, 2007). We are clearly geared toward others from the start. How else could we learn as we do? How else could we expand on what we learn as we do?

Contact with others, through the eyes and other parts of the body, are the vehicles through which we engage others (Tomasello & Carpenter, 2007). Humans are geared to focus quickly and capture the gist of others. This includes their motives, wants, desires, and beliefs. Parts of the brain, such as the amygdala, aid in assessing social context – in getting the gist of something (Adolphs, Denburg, & Tranel, 2001). Fast heuristics in assessing social context must be operative. Getting a sense of something, and generating a toolbox of cognitive and practical tools, is an essential human adaptation (Gigerenzer, 2007; Gigerenzer & Selton, 2001).

In other words, we know that watching and doing can activate many of the same regions of the brain. Frontal and premotor cortices are active at the site of the person who is actually moving (Jackson & Decety, 2004; Jacob & Jeannerod, 2005; Jeannerod, 1999), and these same areas are active when a person is shown words that depict action (Hauk, Johnsrude, & Pulvermuller, 2004). Cognition runs throughout these systems. This is important when considering the educational process and the systems involved in learning from the experiences of others. Thinking of action activates motor regions of the cortex. Again, cognitive systems inhabit all regions of the brain, and no one part of brain is noncognitive (Barton, 2006; Schulkin, 2004, 2007a). Understanding this is important to the comprehension of human action, agency, and adaptation (e.g., Brook & Akins, 2005).

NEURAL PLASTICITY, NEUROGENESIS, AND ENRICHED ENVIRON-
MENTS. Lifelong learning is a rich metaphor for anchoring oneself in the social milieu. Indeed, learning from others should be lifelong. The discovery of neurogenesis, the cellular process of generating new neurons from progenitor cells (Ming & Song, 2005), no doubt is

important for this essential cognitive adaptation and gives physical embodiment to something that we know is important.

A great deal of evidence from animal experiments over the past forty years has demonstrated that enriched environments in both neonates and older animals engender increased neuronal sprouting. This in turn can enhance problem solving (Rosenzweig, 1984). Even simply enriched environments, those with more objects to interact with, engender greater dendritic expression in multiple regions of the brain, including the neocortex, striatum, and hippocampus (Comery et al., 1996; Diamond et al., 1967; Greenough & Volkmar, 1973).

The degree of plasticity in cortical systems is affected by the enriched environment (Klintsova & Greenough, 1999). Learning diverse tasks is found to facilitate synaptogenesis in regions of the brain that include the cerebellar cortex (Black et al., 1990). The formation of synapses in regions of the brain such as the hippocampus can result in long-term potentiation of this region, an area essential for learning and memory formation (McGaugh, 2003).

Neurogenesis (i.e., the expression of new neurons) is something that, for some time, has been known to occur. Recent studies have also demonstrated its occurrence in the adult brains of animals, though neurogenesis decreases with age (Taupin & Gage, 2002). In other words, neurogenesis is expressed in several neural sites (Gould, Reeves, Craziano, & Gross, 1999), and is tied to diverse forms of learning from others (Patton & Nottebohm, 1984). Steroid hormones (e.g., cortisol and estrogen) mediate the effects of events on neuronal expansion and reduction; they prime the brain by facilitating the expression of neuronal gene products (McEwen et al., 1991).

Thus, neurogenesis is tied to adult learning and hippocampal function (Gould et al., 1999; Shors et al., 2001). Moreover, enriched environments promote neurogenesis in the dentate gyrus (Kempermann, Kuhn, & Gage, 1998). In other words, learning promotes both neurogenesis in this region and the long-term potentiation that is critical for that learning (Van Prang, Christie, Sejnowski, & Gage,

1999). The functional significance is the fact that as mammals we are lifelong learners (Abrous, Koehl, & Le Moal, 2005; Kempermann, Wiskott, & Gage, 2004) (see Figure 4.7).

Neurogenesis is a symbolic expression of the long-term regrowth and rejuvenation essential to our species, to our personal lives. Regrowth and regeneration is at the heart of long-term learning. A life like ours, tied to animacy and agency and replete in self-expression, requires this neuronal generation.

CONCLUSION. We come into human society prepared to learn. One of the key ways in which we learn is from focusing on one another's experiences, getting the gist of who they are and the various beliefs and desires they hold, and then using that knowledge in diverse and expanding ways. This ability, along with other cognitive adaptations, is linked to a broad based, self-corrective sense of hypothesis testing. To gain a foothold in the world, we must learn from others and recognize their experiences. To obtain a demythologized Enlightenment perspective, we must embrace self-corrective sensibility amid the sense of others' expression of agency and direction.

The human adventure in education is one of imperfect expression, punctuated by moments of insight. Education cultivates these epiphanies and nurtures their possible continuation. But even without major or minor insights, education cultivates the appreciation of the good, the beautiful, and the true. An experimentalist's sensibility lies amid the humanist's grasp of the myriad ways of trying to understand our existence. To bridge discourse is to appreciate the languages of other cultures, which reveal the nuances of life and experience. Moreover, diverse cognitive resources are endemic to the sensorimotor systems, and the foresight that underlies action may not be particularly conscious.

Cognitive adaptation is rooted in evolution, a world of problem solving and local adaptation (e.g., Rozin, 1976). The predominance of problem-solving abilities is strongly linked to the machinery of

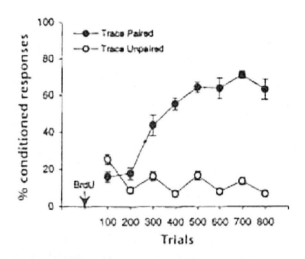

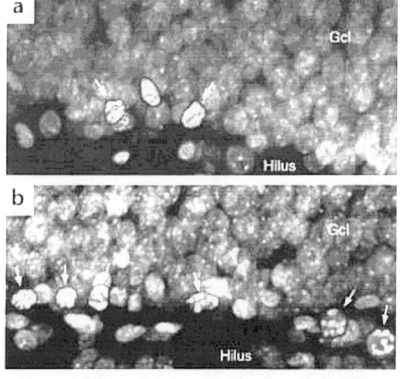

FIGURE 4.7. Induction of learning and neurogenesis (adapted from Gould et al., 1999).

adaptation and is oriented toward coping, striving, and understanding. Cognitive systems are rooted in the worlds that humans inhabit (Clark, 1999; Medin & Atran, 1999, 2004). The evolution of our cognitive abilities is fundamentally linked to the worlds we evolved from and are adapting to, and the worlds we extend by our inventions. The sticks that chimpanzees use and the scopes that we use exemplify all the differences between two species close in genes but far apart in most of what makes us human.

The tools that help us see and hear become part of our evolutionary hardware; the apparently rigid separation between what we make to help us see and hear and what our brain provides is in fact permeable (e.g., Clark, 2003; Wheeler, 2005). The analysis of this niche is as important as the understanding of our mental abilities. The analysis of one without the other is at best banal and at worst misleading.

Among the cardinal features of brain evolution is greater access to and use of the connections between one system and another (Rozin, 1976). Moreover, the extent to which these primitive neuronal systems are accessible to one another is an empirical issue. A function of this greater access to cognitive resources would seem to lie in the ability to further the evolving social intelligence that is characteristic of primates.

Always present is a fundamental adaptation of our species: linking up with others. Of course, Fortuna and hard work go hand and hand. Diverse regions of the brain underlie this ability to learn from the experiences of others, to share knowledge, to evolve into a pedagogical individual. Amid this are regions of the brain that generate neurogenesis. We thrive on meaningful connections with others (Jaspers, 1913/1997). Education figures in the quest to integrate the messianic ideal of the utopian supportive community within the context of freedom of individual expression. It becomes ever more important to instill a deep political sense in our citizens through the study of history. Educational sensibilities transcend national borders (see Nussbaum,

1997). Thus, the educated are not just well versed in the expression of intelligence, from rhetoric to mathematical knowledge, but they seek wisdom. Wisdom is tied to an appreciation and an understanding of experiences other than one's own (e.g., Jaspers, 1951, 1954; Happe et al., 1998; Johnson, 1993; Neville, 1992; Schulkin, 1992).

5

An Instinct for Spiritual Quests: Quiet Religion

Any one of our beliefs is subject to criticism, revision and even ultimate elimination through the development of its own implications by intelligently directed action.
– John Dewey, *The Influence of Darwin on Philosophy*

INTRODUCTION. Spiritual quests are not an aberration or a pathological state. They are, rather, a fundamental need. Moreover, conversions to "seeing" events in a certain way are at the basis of scientific and other forms of experience, as are spiritual quests (Heelan, 1994).

Importantly, as John Dewey (1934/1970) noted in his book *A Common Faith*, "any activity pursued in behalf of an ideal end against obstacles and in spite of threats of personal loss because of conviction of its general and enduring value is religious in quality" (p. 27). What is important is to provide sustenance for what is valuable and alive (see also Kitcher, 2007). Particularly in an age of theological fundamentalism, self-corrective inquiry, a commitment to nonviolence, and humility serve as useful adjuncts to any investigation of religious belief.

Religious quests are vital human activities and cut across both the sciences and the humanities. Religious sensibility is one thing; religious tyranny is quite another. Religious sensibility, at its normative best, is humble and pluralistic. The approach that I suggest avoids dismissive positivism and dogmatic theological fundamentalism to favor a pious naturalism.

My argument is that religious sensibility – a basic human predilection – needs to be knotted to self-corrective inquiry and humility to avoid religious tyranny, which is no easy chore. Self-corrective inquiry requires strong pedagogy amid innate predilection. What underlies spiritual quests are (1) heightened vigilance and some discomfort or unrest about human existence, (2) a search to come to terms with this fact, and (3) the much-appreciated moments of peace and quietude needed for human well-being. What is important is to bring ideas to the lifeblood of experience, to the everyday, to bring the conception of vulnerability and hypothesis-testing inquiry to cover the whole range of human experience, including spiritual inquiry.

In what follows, I first suggest that spiritual quests are fundamental to the human condition and then that certain cognitive categories and basic instinctive responses predispose us to express this human need, underlaid by the activity of diverse brain regions.

A CONCEPTION OF SPIRITUAL QUESTS. Spiritual quests are an important part of the human condition, to be cultivated in human development; the question is, "How to naturalize such events and tie them to self-corrective inquiry when possible?" Spiritual quests begin, perhaps, like most forms of inquiry – tinged with doubt and self-reflection. Inquiry, as Peirce (1878/1992) noted, is to help, in part, to quell doubt, taper it, and place it in perspective. In Peirce's words, "the irritation of doubt causes a struggle to attain a state of belief, I shall term this struggle inquiry" (p. 114); what emerges is the search for a semblance of satisfaction to ameliorate the irritation.

The first phase of any spiritual quest is knotted to appetitive behaviors; search engines permeate sense experience and most forms of inquiry. The second phase reflects consummatory behaviors – the sense of accomplishment, goal achievement, the securing of some sense of satiation. A number of investigators mark the appetitive and consummatory phases of experience as fundamental to our basic mode of existence (Craig, 1918; Dewey, 1925/1989). I suggest that this distinction also underlies spiritual quests and spiritual inquiry.

Although, anti-theism of any sort is more than a defensible position amid religious dogmatism and, worse, religious tyranny (e.g., Dawkins, 2006; Dennett, 2006; Hume, 1757/1957; Kitcher, 2007), there is a basic human need for spiritual quests that we should acknowledge and link to self-corrective inquiry and humility. An important expression of a humble spiritual quest is replete with nonviolence; Gandhi (1964) noted that, perhaps, "if we remain non-violent, hatred will die as everything does, from disuse" (p. 43).

An important distinction exists between spirituality and religion – and spirituality is an important component of the human condition (e.g., asking about the meaning of life, finding pathways to address that sort of question). Religion, on the other hand, usually reflects settled practices (Durkheim, 1915/1965). Why do we need spiritual inquiry? Our sense of religion and our spiritual life are about those things that are of ultimate concern (Tillich, 1951/1967), such as the bonds we form with one another, and, ultimately, meaning (James, 1896/1956; Jaspers, 1913/1997). As Karl Jaspers (1913/1997) stated, "We are always being led by ideas to a complex unity of meaningful connections" (p. 760). The continued search for meaning underlies human existence.

But the spiritual quest is existentially rooted in some discomfort, and the search to quell this unease reflects an appetitive phase of spiritual inquiry. This is an unease for which Søren Kierkegaard (1844/1980) noted that "all existence" (p. 170), at some level, renders one anxious and requires resolution. Such resolutions might be big, splashy affairs, revolutions really: Martin Luther hammering his theses onto a church door, Ezra addressing the Israelites returned from Babylon. But cultural evolution in religious expression has tended to constitute something I call "quiet religion." Quiet religion requires us to investigate the strengths of various religious traditions. Not surprisingly, at the heart of quiet religion lies inquiry and freedom.

Freedom to engage in spiritual quests and their expression has been at the heart of one part of our culture, as well as wonder about ourselves and our evolution, and a pious attitude toward nature, with the normative goal of greater depth of character (e.g., Dewey, 1934; Whitehead, 1938/1967).

The spiritual life lives in the flesh, in the body, and in the cultural ambiance that one breathes in diverse forms of cognitive adaptation (Barsalou, Barbey, Simmons, & Satos, 2005; Johnson & Rohrer, 2007; Lakoff & Johnson, 1999; Varela, Thompson, & Rosch, 1991). Humans are part of nature, having evolved as part of it. Human beings share a common biological bond with other animals, and various studies of social primates indicate that social bonds are essential for infant survival. Elaborate social intelligence and bonding (Humphrey, 1976), amid complex cognitive forms of cooperation and deception, is a common element in hominoid evolution (De Waal, 2000).

Quiet religion cultivates naturalism. Saint Francis of Assisi's love of birds was a deep spiritual union. Zen masters' unity and prowess in nature is real. Images of Mother Earth capture the liveliness of nature (see Figure 5.1). As Immanuel Kant (1792/1951) said, the great majority of sublime nature demythologized is a real fact (see also Oelschlaeger, 1991). Nature demythologized recognizes our fundamental evolutionary link to nature, the inherent regeneration and rebirth so richly and diversely expressed in nature.

Not all philosophy has been friendly to the spiritual quest, however. For the Epicureans and Lucretius, through to David Hume, Baruch Spinoza, and many radical Enlightenment thinkers, religion meant superstition. The positivists made it seem like spiritual quests were cognitively meaningless. But they are forms of human expression that are inherently knotted to cognitive systems. Although religion can indeed numb the intellect, or provide a search for a great womb or a parental figure to provide omniscient protection and comfort (e.g., Freud, 1927/1964), it need not do so. Rather, the spiritual is the call to be awakened; to be attentive to the common bonds in

FIGURE 5.1. Saint Francis with the birds, and a meditator (Yansen & Schulkin, 2007).

humanity; to be tolerant, as John Locke (1692–1704) understood it to be; to collapse the barriers among us; to extend a hand; and to cultivate sacred humanity as a way of life.

The sense of a worthy event, "perpetual peace" (Kant, 1792/1951, p. 30), is a religious normative goal for which many of us strive; it reflects the consummatory phase of the experience of religious inquiry. This is an essential end point of quiet religion. Amid the recognition of tragedy, struggle, and turmoil, the glimmer of peace creates great joy. The place of peace is one of a shared humanity, a place where all are welcome. Expressed in the words of an African American spiritual, "No one will throw me out."

The sense of peace is that kingdom of moral ends that Kant (1788/1956) describes, where we treat one another as full human

beings, or as *thou* rather than *it*, as the theologian Martin Buber
(1937/1970) expressed it. That is, people are treated with dignity, and
their worth recognized, appreciated, cultivated, and loved. We are a
species with a great need to belong, to form social contact, to create
symbolic systems to respect our ancestors (King, 2007). This great fantasy of everlasting peaceful coexistence is a worthy myth. It is deeply
tied to the spiritual bonds that keep humans afloat amid the turbulence of life and nature. Erich Fromm (1950/1972), in the foreword
to one of his books on religion, makes a relevant point as he quotes
Abbé Pire: "What matters is not the difference between believers and
unbelievers, but between those who care and those who do not care"
(p. 2).

The joy of wonder, of permanent peace and love, emerges often
in ephemeral moments. The issue of religious inquiry, and whether
what one finds is good, is empirical – and this means living with the
hypothetical nature of our spiritual beliefs while recognizing their
importance to human sensibility. Humility, from this perspective, is
both an important tool and a vital end point (Neville, 1992; Peirce,
1908/1998).

CATEGORIES OF THE HOLY: NATURE AND CULTURE. Spirituality is
a fundamental characteristic of human beings. It is so much a part
of us that it may be akin to our capacity for syntactic competence or
language use: a species-specific behavior. Spiritual expression is something that only we possess in the animal kingdom; to our knowledge,
no other animal is spiritual. Many scholars have noted the "naturalness of the religious motives" (Royce, 1912/1940, p. 42; see also Rue,
2005), yet no other species worships or formulates spiritual quests.

Perhaps we humans uniquely possess a set of categories (classes
of representations linked together) about divine events. A category of
the "holy" would be presupposed, along with the social practices and
rituals that we participate in, for having our spiritual experiences, a
sense of the "numinous" (Otto, 1923, /1975), and which might increase

the probability of treating one another in the context of what Kant or Buber described – the sense of an animate objects with beliefs and, desires, and a sense of agency worthy of respect and dignity.

Such evolutionally favorable categories may predispose us toward spiritual experiences, and such predispositions may, in turn, be part of our hunger for knowledge. It is a faculty akin to that of syntax and other cognitive orientations (Atran, 2002; Boyer, 1994). Diverse religious expressions may reflect the activation of a cognitive competence knotted to a basic orientation, just as in language itself, in which there are multiple expressions set by linguistic structure (Levinson, 2006; Pinker, 1994). Categories of the supernatural are, after all, more readily expressed than are those of science (Barrett & Keil, 1996; Bloom, 2007; McCauley, 2000). People perhaps have a predilection to form religious beliefs based on basic categories of the mind. The ease with which we do so across cultures and the expression of this formation early in individual development suggest that a cognitive category of "holy" is a natural part of us.

One significant cognitive adaptation for the expression of religious sensibility is the attribution of desires and beliefs (Atran, 2002). Because this intentional stance is fairly pervasive, we tend to extend it to nonhuman agents. The cognitive science of religion reveals that we attribute intentions, beliefs, and desires to superhuman agents (Barrett & Keil, 1996), a predilection that we have derived from our cognitive arsenal.

Our everyday psychological categories, such as agency or animacy, in addition to biological categories (Carey & Gelman, 1991; Keil, 1979), may interact with the representational capacity for religious expression. Features of spirituality often take two properties: (1) superhuman agency (though not all religions require this; Barrett, 2000; Barrett & Keil, 1996) and (2) a sense of both supreme agency beyond what we experience ourselves and universal and originatory animacy, the fundamental well of life. As I have indicated in previous chapters, young children have some understanding of these categories early in life (Carey & Gelman, 1991; Keil, 1979). They are expressed across a wide range of cultures (Boyer & Ramble, 2001), and both categories figure in the organization of human cognitive capacities (Keil, 1979, 2007).

Religious representations, when experimentally challenged, often tend to be anthropomorphic in nature (though, again, not all religions are anthropomorphic). An experiment by Barrett and Keil (1996) directly addressed this issue by constructing short vignettes to access the conceptions of God from subjects of different religious backgrounds. Most study participants tended to anthropomorphize the concept of God across experimental paradigms, independent of their religious or nonreligious predilections. Different cognitive explanations of religious ideas also suggest that people readily anthropomorphize and naturalize intuitive concepts of divinity. In several studies involving people of different backgrounds and religions, subjects readily used anthropomorphic concepts of divinity to understand stories, despite their predilection or personal theological position (Boyer & Ramble, 2001).

It seems that we come prepared to see the world around us in religious terms; it is in part a reflection of our cognitive machinations. More generally, cognitive systems underlie religious rituals (Lawson & McCauley, 1990; McCauley & Lawson, 2002). It is not an aberration to capture a mystical sense of the world, to be awestruck by the material features of nature, by our inability to fully capture our surroundings. We perhaps use categories derived from folk psychology (agency) and folk biology (animism) for religious representations. Religious sensibility is as natural to us as is eating apples. The ontological features vary, and an extension of our cognitive predilections may be misleading in its application to issues that speak of the religious – the naturalness of unnatural claims (McCauley, 2000). Diverse forms of cognitive preconditions set the terms for religious inquiry (Atran, 2002; Boyer, 1994), for spiritual quests. Most important, a sense of purpose runs through spiritual quests.

However, a vast array of religious quests do not contain a godlike agent (e.g., Taoism, Buddhism; Neville, 1992). For example, one noted Western scholar, in commenting on Buddhism, noted the following: "it has been seriously maintained that Buddhism is not religion at all because it denies God. This it certainly does, but it is nevertheless religion, for it lives in the numinous. The salvation sought in Nirvana like that sought in Yoga is magical and numinous" (Otto, 1952/1972, p. 100). A normative goal for both theistic and atheistic belief systems is a sense of quiet, attentive peace as the desired end of a quest permeated by disciplined discovery.

In some traditions, a sense of nature is pervasive, as one acknowledges "the great machinery (of evolution) from which all things come forth (at birth) and which they enter at death" (Chan, 1963; Tzu, 1962). These traditions certainly contain a keen sense of nature as alive – and I would suggest that a sense of animacy underlies almost all spiritual quests. Consider this seductive statement from the Buddha: "The way is perfect like unto vast space, with nothing wanting, nothing superfluous" (Conze, 1951/1975, 1959/1984).

AN INSTINCT FOR SPIRITUAL QUESTS. Peirce (1893/1936) speculated that perhaps we have an instinct for religious quests, as basic to us as syntax. Humans certainly have a predilection for religious expression. The concept of instinct figured importantly for Darwin (1871/1874). The issue that permeated biology and psychobiology was the relationship between what is inherited and what is acquired (e.g., James, 1887; Rozin, 1976). Darwin noted that species-specific behavioral and physiological adaptations are richly expressed and tied, perhaps, to finding sources of energy, to primary motivational systems and their release in suitable environments.

In The Descent of Man, Darwin (1871/1874), as is very well known, compared human evolution to that of other species (see Figure 5.2). He suggested that "the fewness and the comparative simplicity of the instincts in the higher animals are remarkable in contrast with those of

FIGURE 5.2. Charles Darwin.

the lower animals" (p. 65). We instinctually learn some things rapidly (Marler, 2000; Rozin, 1976), such as learning from other people's experiences.

Spiritual inquiry within quiet religion emphasizes an appreciation of the natural world and our tie to it. John Muir captured it as he described the splendor of Yosemite Park. Henry Thoreau described it in his solitary walks in the woods. Many inquirers, including Thoreau and Ralph Waldo Emerson, have described the spiritual sense of being part of nature.

Since the Enlightenment, we have often separated spirituality from nature. However, in my view, spiritual inquiry binds nature and culture together. Emerson (1855/1883), among many others, captured the

FIGURE 5.3. Yosemite (Yansen & Schulkin, 2007).

divinity in nature and the important spiritual experiences one has in being part of nature (see Figure 5.3). A natural theology lay imminent in this approach, one that emphasizes inquiry and an appreciation of nature. Amid this sensibility is, as William James (1902/1974) suggested, a rendering of these spiritual investigations as empirical, for the predisposition for such inquiry is part of our psychological constitution.

The separation of nature and spirit is misguided. The noted scholar Mircea Eliade (1957) observed that, often for a person on a spiritual quest, "nature is never only natural, it is always fraught with religious value" (p. 116). A sense of nature is a very important experience, something one needs (e.g., Oelschlaeger, 1991; Schulkin, 1996). Mother Earth (Bachofen, 1967; Malinowski, 1948) and her power resides there: values, ethics and duties that one has to preserve the ecosphere; to reinterpret nature anew as alive, not dead and inert; and to return to what has been called Magna Mater (Oelschlaeger, 1991). To lose this tie to nature is to lose something very important, a sense of the world as alive (Whitehead, 1938/1967). We evolved with nature, and now we evolve further toward a common humanity (e.g., human rights; Sarokin & Schulkin, 1994), resurrecting the bond we have with nature and ourselves. Our common humanity and our fundamental tie to nature are ever present. Some of us view nature as truly alive but with a shared sense of humanity (Nussbaum, 1997). We are deeply part of nature, and this experience involves a strong sense of human dignity. It also requires humility and perseverance. For a Buddhist, this sensibility is compassion (Conze, 1951/1975).

But still, a cautionary note: our limitations abound (e.g., biological, emotional, intellectual, and spiritual ones). One is bound, yet one glimpses great majesty – the majesty of divine peaceful reciprocity. A sense of wonder and mystery, that spiritual warmth that holds one together, is pervasive, but there are times when the spiritual quest leads one into a vast desert, what Saint John of the Cross called "the dark night of the soul." That dark night, that desert, is as much a part of the spiritual quest as a sense of oneness with nature. We are, after all, alone. Spiritual peace and insights require the realization of the individual's aloneness.

The spiritual sense of quiet religion is one of process, of action, of enlarging human experiences, and this of course reflects the appetitive or search phase of religious inquiry. It was what James (1902/1974) put in the context of the healthy minded, though some would suggest that such activities are dependent upon anxiety (Kierkegaard, 1844/1980). But faith emerges from the anxiety, the confrontation of finitude. There is a gentler way to experience this freedom of dynamic religion that requires a balancing of contrast, an ability to engage the precarious but not be done in by it. The humanness that can emerge and predominate is embedded in the ceremonies of worldly wisdom and spontaneity. Quiet religion implies acceptance and stoicism. Humility and thankfulness are the dominant sensibilities. Forgiveness provides constant renewal and restoration to offer hope and to move on. After all, many positive emotions are linked to a perceived sense of awe – to a sense that objects are unlimited (Haidt, 2006; Keltner & Haidt, 2003).

The instinct for religion or faith must also be anchored to ideals worthy of our human condition, humbled by our vulnerability to abuse one another. John Dewey (1934), for instance, was interested in preserving the sense of religious questions but not the foundational forms of religion (see also Flanagan, 2007).

QUIET RELIGION: AN EXPERIMENTAL STATE OF MIND. An active sense of problem was part of classical pragmatism, which was rooted in biology (see Godfrey-Smith, 2002; Smith, 1978) and knotted to an experimental state of mind. Pragmatism extended this attitude to religious predilections, and part of my argument is that this is important as a small prophylactic against religious fundamentalism. This experimental state of mind holds that (1) claims are hypothetical, (2) a rich set of representational systems are presupposed, and (3) diverse regions of the brain underlie the expression of spiritual quests. This state of mind does not mean, of course, that the same methods are used to determine the utility of the truth-value of religious claims. It would be nice to see religious expression toned down, humbled yet strengthened, by an experimental state of mind, to discern more clearly the hypothetical nature of our spiritual views and to place spiritual quests amid a larger sense of self-corrective inquiry (e.g., Neville, 1992; Solomon, 2002).

Bodily rituals underlie religious expression (Atran, 2002). The sense of being embodied as an individual is often a characteristic of religious expression. Push aside the Cartesian conception of divorced mind from body as the only dominant conception of the mind and what is left are diverse adaptations and experiences by agents, individuals making sense of their world; it is then that the sense of mind in body takes on real validity (e.g., Damasio, 1996; Lakoff & Johnson,

1999; Prinz, 2004; Schulkin, 2004). Sets of representational capabilities, linked to agency and desire, are a fundamental property of the brain (Decety, 1996; Decety & Jackson, 2006).

Cognition pervades human experience. It is not as if the body is on one side and cognitive systems on the other (Lakoff & Johnson, 1999; Merleau-Ponty, 1942/1967; Schulkin, 2000, 2004). All of these actions are rich in cognitive resources, particularly the sense of embodied cognition, which is so important for spiritual quests (Barsalou et al., 2005; Varela et al., 1991).

A healthy sense of the mind in the body (e.g., agency and animacy in quiet religion) can be achieved, for example, by the practice of Tai Chi Chuan or yoga (e.g., Delza, 1961/1985) (see Figure 5.4). The rituals are well composed, and the goals are clear. The spiritual sensibility, normatively, is tied to the organization of action and to quiet acts of compassion.

Regions of the frontal cortex are essential for a number of higher-order functions, including syntax (Ullman, 2001) and perhaps the organization of religious rituals; the motor programs are highly cognitive, which is why we call them rituals (McCauley & Lawson, 2002). Religious expressions also reflect differential regions of the brain. Areas such as the amygdala and the frontal and temporal cortices may be influential in the basic desire for religious expression. Regions of the frontal cortex and basal ganglia may also be fundamental to the organization of religious rites. These regions in diverse contexts have been linked to discharges of religious expressions, from kindling-like effects in the amygdala to representations of objects, some seen and some not (Gloor, 1997).

Sharing rituals may mean sharing a neural signature both in what I do and in what I watch you do. Diverse regions of the brain, including the amygdala and the larger temporal cortex and frontal cortex have, in many studies, been linked to religious sensibility (Russell, Murphy, Meyering, & Arbib, 2002; Saver & Rabin, 1997; Wuerfel et al., 2004). For instance, regions of the frontal cortex appear to be

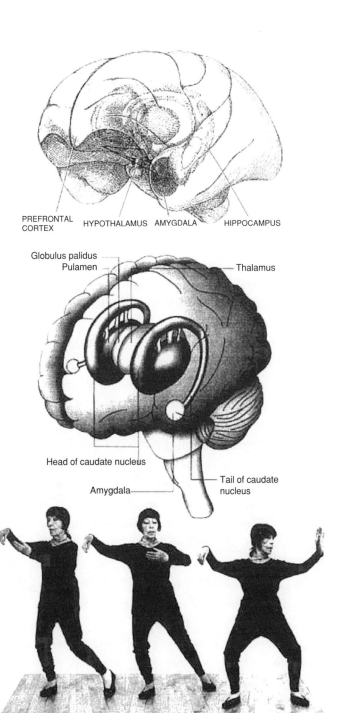

FIGURE 5.4. The practice of Tai Chi and several regions of the brain that underlie the organization of such practices.

differentially activated during ritualized meditation (Davidson et al., 2003; Lutz, Greischar, Rawling, Ricard, & Davidson, 2004). The left frontal cortex, which is linked to positive affect, is greater in expression following ritualized meditation. Meditation is not a passive state but a quiet state of reflection. In other words, regions of the brain that are linked to positive emotion are active during states of meditation (Austin, 2006). Zen and others forms of meditation also are known to promote greater immune function; meditation promotes immunologic defense. This same sense of meditation has long been linked to states of enlightenment, of grasping things of concern, and to increased compassion and attention to detail. Meditation is strongly tied to well-being and a broad array of positive emotions (Davidson et al., 2003; Ekman, Davidson, Ricard, & Wallace, 2005; Fromm, Suzuki, & DeMartino, 1960/1970; Harrington & Zajonc, 2006) (see Figure 5.5).

In states of meditation, quiet focus is a profound state of rejuvenation of the brain, and hormones such as prolactin promote neurogenesis in the brain. One set of hormones signals activation (e.g., cortisol, the wake-up hormone) and the other quiescence (e.g., prolactin). Translated into the brain, regions such as the amygdala contain chemical signals (neuropeptide hormones) that quiet one, as well as those that arouse one or orient one toward disruption (Herbert & Schulkin, 2002; Schulkin, 1999).

From an evolutionary point of view, meditative states perhaps have roots in those periods in our evolutionary history when we sat quietly, maybe during the transition between daylight hours and nighttime; a time of transition when it was not light out but we were not asleep. This would constitute a resting state, perhaps evolving into a reflective state. Hormones, such as prolactin, are known in humans to be secreted during the dark phase, particularly during the transition between light and darkness (Wehr et al., 1993; Wehr & Schulkin, 1995, unpublished). Prolactin, like melatonin (another

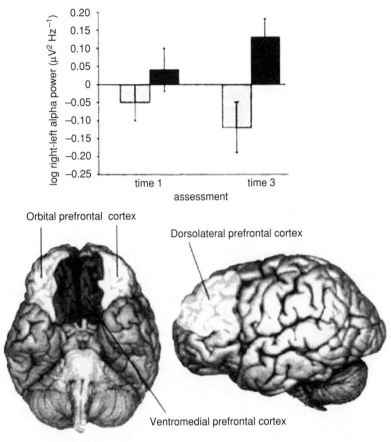

FIGURE 5.5. Regions of the brain implicated in experienced meditators (adapted from Davidson et al., 2003).

hormone), is known to be involved in the transduction from light-related activities to a more quiescent state (Wehr et al., 1993) (see Figure 5.6).

Possibly before the onset of the modern period, with its chronic lights, there were quiet periods in which we were not asleep but at rest. Perhaps this is reflected in the quiet wakefulness experienced by pre-electric-light societies (Sterling, 2004; Sterling & Eyer, 1988).

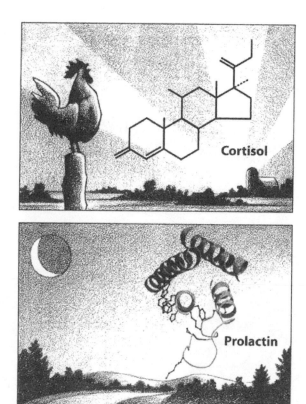

FIGURE 5.6. The morning-linked hormone cortisol and evening-relaxation-linked prolactin (Yansen & Schulkin, 2007).

Importantly, there is evidence that experienced meditators have higher levels of prolactin during meditation than do those who are less experienced. In several studies, prolactin release was elevated (Jevning, Wilson, & VanderLaan, 1978; Wehr & Schulkin, 1995, unpublished). Meditative states are restorative states, states of quiescence, and perhaps hormones such as prolactin evolved from a functional role in the transition from activity to rest. Moreover, hormones such as prolactin are, in birds, linked to brooding behavior (Lehrman, 1958) – sitting on those eggs motionless for long periods of time.

CONCLUSION. The spiritual life lives in the flesh and in the cultural ambiance that one breathes. Regions of the brain linked to needs, in this case spiritual needs, are recruited in the expression of spiritual inquiry. The amygdala is well suited to serve this function because it underlies a number of drives that we have. What William James called a "faith state" is part of our psychobiological constitution. The amygdala, hippocampus, and diverse neocortical systems underlie spiritual inquiry (Muramoto, 2004; Russell et al., 2002; Saver & Rabin, 1997; Wuerfel et al., 2004). Spiritual inquiry, I would suggest, is vital for our self-development. This chapter has indicated that the basic predilection for religious expression needs to be knotted to self-corrective inquiry and humility – even more so in the face of religious fundamentalism. Quiet religion, and what I suggest it entails, does not mean silence. But it does speak of inquiry. I have suggested that two phases of human experience underlie spiritual inquiry: an appetitive phase knotted to search and a consummatory phase linked to quiet peacefulness. They can be expressed in the thundering of the most rhapsodic gospel chant, in the Quaker and Buddhist traditions of silence, or in the movements and calls of Jewish davening. Quiet religion speaks directly to those who are spiritual but who do not have a set of religious beliefs to ascribe to, a set of doctrines instantiated in practice (e.g., Fromm, 1947; Rorty, 1999; Spinoza, 1668/1955).

Indeed, a sense of inquiry should be at the heart of such a quest, but inquiry is not enough. For the spiritual life has to do with gentle offerings in the face of harsh realities. The spiritual quests are manifest in diverse settings; for James it was linked to a spiritual moment amid the recognition that good does not always prevail.

Near the end of his book *The Varieties of Religious Experience*, William James (1902/1974) characterizes the positive psychological characteristics of religious quests as including the following: (1) "A new zest, which adds itself like a gift to life, and takes the form either of lyrical enhancement or of appeal to earnestness and heroism," and (2) "An assurance of safety and temper of peace and in relation to others, a preponderance of loving affections" (p. 377). We now know a bit about the cognitive basis of religious expression. Cognitive capacities that reflect folk psychology (agency, intentionality) and folk biology (animacy) appear to be two cognitive resources that render religious expressions possible.

James (1902/1974) overemphasized the extreme and sensory aspects of religious experience, but he shows that cognitive penetration pervades all parts of human expression, religious or otherwise. There are no simple givens in any aspect of life, except the historical givens of our experiences, what we are exposed to, the historical contingencies, the practices we participate in because of what confronts us. The rich social life of human experience pervades, as do various forms of understanding on which we rely. Our turn to the spiritual for sustenance emerges, in part, from the insecurity and uncertainty of human existence amid a set of cognitive preconditions.

It is nearly impossible to give defining characteristics for natural categories, but two features of quiet religion stand out: a sense of awe is made manifest in the face of a pervasive sense of animacy and agency. Religious sensibility is also demythologized, placed in a self-corrective context. Its root is in diverse cognitive abilities, some of which have to do with our sense of biology, to a naturalized sense of the world, at times extended beyond what is intelligible.

Of course, there is more than one way to generate the gentleness of the community of living citizens, caretakers, and concerned individuals awed by the miracle of communion of humanity. Quiet religion stresses that ultimate matters are found in a variety of forms and that inquiry should predominate.

Normatively, science and other pursuits in the humanities are engaged, reflected on, and mused about. Individual enlightenment integrates (or does not) those forms into a responsible spiritual fabric. But as Taylor (2002, 2007) has noted, echoing a philosophical sentiment that has been voiced by others, there is a tension between the personal sense of religious quests and the descent into self-absorption and shallowness. Our social bonds, our respect for one another and for worthy ends, need also to be anchored to the spiritual quests in which being thoughtful is a normative goal (Solomon, 2002).

Competition for survival is a factor of evolution. So is the binding Eros of spiritual *Homo sapiens*. The trajectory is dependent on what Peirce called "evolutionary love." But in an age when theological fundamentalism and political and social arrogance are still common phenomena, when theological dogmatic seduction is the common currency, quiet religion necessitates growing roots in human bonds. Religious sentiments ought to be based on compassion toward one another (e.g., Davidson & Harrington, 2002; Fromm, Suzuki, & De Martino, 1960/1970). The achievement is ephemeral and awe inspiring. Peace is felt, dignity is revealed, and benevolence effervesces – and then it may be gone. But the moment is preserved in memory.

In summary, spiritual quests are fundamental to the human condition, perhaps an instinctive feature of us that reflects both search (quest) and consummation (a sense of peace). Two cognitive categories contribute significantly to the expression of spiritual quests: animacy and agency. The first is knotted to categorical depictions of classes and relations of living things, and the second to the sense and recognition of individual aspirations. Both figure importantly in spiritual quests and should be linked to self-corrective inquiry, not to fundamentalist authority-based religious expressions. Only then does a worthy sense of human expression manifest.

Conclusion

Demythologized Reason

so much depends
upon

a red wheel
barrow

glazed with rain
water

beside the white
chickens.
– William Carlos Williams, "The Red Wheelbarrow"

The human condition is determined on the one hand by our evolutionary history and on the other by pervading historical and social factors. We are thrust out in the world. The process of evolution engendered in humans a desire to compete and to cooperate, to form bonds of intimacy – and to deceive.

To placate the uncertainty and insecurity of existence, science has in some ways replaced the traditional theologies that attempted to satisfy our quest for certainty (Dewey, 1929/1960). Human desire for certain knowledge and boundless security is infinite in scope. Our aspirations rise higher than any barometer we can construct. Whatever science is, it is not about certainty but knowledge. And it does represent one of the glorious treasures of humankind.

A sense of history matters, not because all theories are equally as real but because history, our conception of ourselves, continues to change (Fuller, 1998; Kuhn, 2000). Science, like everything else human, is historically contingent (Dear, 1995, 2006; Hull, 1988; Shapin, 1995, 1996; Todes, 1989, 1997) and always needs to be linked to what matters to the human condition (Polanyi, 1946/1964). Perhaps a phrase from Kuhn is applicable: "post Darwinian/Kantianism" (Kuhn, 2000, p. 164), enriched by lexical entries in the common vocabulary of understanding (Levinson & Jaisson, 2006).

Because we are social animals linked with others, our evolutionary history shows a propensity to achieve conflict resolution (De Waal, 2000). Appraisal mechanisms of oneself and others are inherent, and they are expressed early (Kagan, 1984/2002) and in closely related species (Cheney & Seyfarth, 1990, 2007; Hauser, 2000); cooperation is essential in all primates. But deception and the evolution of the arms race also are closely associated with our evolutionary past and with our cultural and historical evolution.

It is the sense of the life world with others, and in our transactions, that theory and practice in everyday life in the sciences is to be uncovered (e.g., Dewey, 1925/1989; Heelan & Schulkin, 1998). These events are both existential and historical, and should be knotted to self-corrective methods of inquiry and hypothesis testing as broadly conceived across the spectrum of human experience, from art to religion. Central metaphors define our approaches to inquiry (e.g., Galison, 1988); our cognitive arsenal provides the orientation and the set of skills (Carey, 2004; Lakoff & Johnson, 1999).

ANIMACY AND AGENCY DEMYTHOLOGIZED IN PREPARED COGNITIVE SYSTEMS. We are prepared to see the world with animacy and agency as dominant categories, just as we come prepared to associate the taste of certain foods with gastrointestinal distress. Prepared kinds of learning set the background in which education and learning from others take place (Rozin, 1976). The conception of a demythologized nature allows us to recognize our roots in evolution in the natural world; that does not denigrate the all-pervasive cultural features that permeate our existence.

Nature alive is a full-fledged ideal of William Wordsworth and Alfred North Whitehead, nature coming into being and perishing; in the works of Henry Thoreau and Charles Darwin, nature is realized as part of the human spirit and evolutionary legacy. Nature demythologized is the full recognition of the omnipresent dangers of our creations, the Frankensteins that linger, neutral with regard to their being but not with regard to their use. The concept of agency is put into perspective when it finds expression in everyday considerations, in our activities, in learning, in history, in religious quests.

Nature alive and demythologized recognizes that our memory of events is rooted in the landscapes into which we are born (Schama, 1995). Demythologized sensibility is not dispirited or reduced to barren rationality, rationality without passion. Embodied cognitive systems are endemic to central nervous system function; the brain is an information-processing system, a diverse collection of systems that reflect the cognitive machinations of the brain (Schulkin, 2004).

The idea of embodied cognitive systems requires two concepts – a sense of animacy and a sense of agency – key cognitive categories that underlie our sense of one another, of ourselves, and that figure in our understanding of human history (Bandura, 2006) (see Figure C.1). The origins of our psychology are perhaps found in the fundamental distinction between animate and inanimate objects. Core knowledge, such as these two categories, permeates the cognitive architecture, including concepts about physical objects living and nonbiological, causation, and orientation toward others –their experiences, expectations, and intentions. The classificatory distinction of the living from the nonliving is a fundamental cognitive adaptation much expanded and developed. Categorical attributions of animacy and agency are dominant early but not totally unconstrained (Gelman, 2003), and they are intertwined. Both categories matter in determining the world around us (e.g., Atran, 1990/1996; Boyer, 2002).

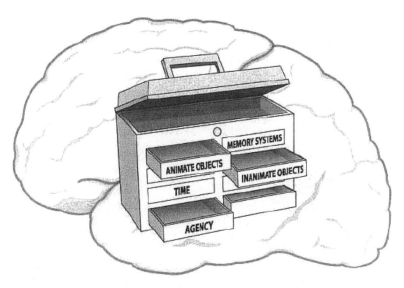

FIGURE C.1. Toolbox of understanding (Yansen & Schulkin, 2005, unpublished).

ENDLESS BOOTSTRAPPING: INQUIRY WITHOUT FRILLS. Epistemic diversity, like biological diversity, is both the reality of the scientific enterprise and an adaptation of it. A combination of instruments, experiments, and theory cut across the range of inquiry (Dear, 2006; Galison, 1988, 1999; Heelan, 2001; Shapin, 1996). In this age of information, our dependence on and trust in one another as scientists is essential for meaningful inquiry. Scientists working on different aspects of the same project generally have a certain level of ignorance of one another's specialties (see Figure C.2). The Renaissance man of earlier centuries, who could embody the knowledge of an era, is no longer with us, if such a person indeed ever existed. Today's scope of scientific knowledge is far too vast for one person to completely embrace, and hence the emergence of specialties and subspecialties in science and medicine. In an era of exponential leaps in scientific knowledge, the multiple levels of analysis required in the scientific enterprise necessitate that we work together, because the knowledge

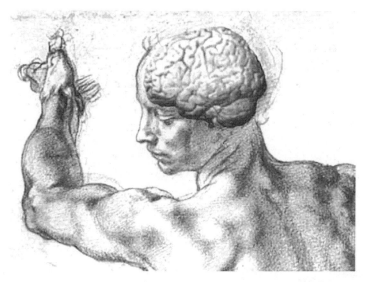

FIGURE C.2. Reaching (Michelangelo, adapted by Yansen & Schulkin, 2007; see Linas, 2001).

of each level is not – indeed, cannot possibly be – shared by all members of the group

So, in addition to inherent competition, collaborative bonds, the recognition of others, and our link to them is essential to advances in knowledge. As Peirce (1883, 1898/1992) would say, a "laboratory frame of mind" is at the heart of this endeavor. Peirce, an essential pragmatist thinker, established a philosophy of self-correction and set up the first experimental laboratory in psychophysics in America. He understood that all experience is embedded in practices that are rich with frames of reference (e.g., Hanson, 1958; Heelan & Schulkin, 1998; Giere, 2006); as we perceive the world around us, we presuppose background sets of inferences. These inferences are often not conscious or even necessarily accessible, but they pervade our biological adaptation and set the conditions for scientific reasoning (Rozin, 1976).

Any form of inquiry needs to be self-corrective. Assumptions must be questioned; biases permeate any endeavor and their recognition is

TABLE C.1.

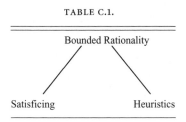

an important factor. Moreover, the recognition of biases in human decision making functions by what social scientists call "sensitizing concepts," which provides a context to understand how we decide. Some of these biases are simple, rough heuristics that work well, have been selected by evolutionary factors, and are part of our cognitive apparatus. Multiple cognitive systems operate across the many areas of inquiry that we pursue (see Rozin, 1976; Simon, 1962).

Research in the decision sciences reinforced a shift to the logic of heuristics in reasoning, or what Herb Simon (1962, 1982; see also Gigerenzer & Selten, 2001) called "satisficing" – what has also been called "bounded rationality." All decision making reflects the frameworks out of which one interprets one's world, amid the lifeworld in which one participates, breathes the air. The mantle of perfect reason inherited from the Enlightenment (Israel, 2001) is replaced with demythologized reason, problem solving rooted in human experience, existential and pragmatic (Cherniak, 1986; Dayes, 2001) – less than perfect decision making – concerning the choices of everyday life (see Table C.1).

The demythologizing of decision making, whether within philosophy or within psychology, requires that one take hold of the fact that science works and that there are advances to be proud of, but that human reasoning, scientific or otherwise, is replete with flaws. The realization that optimization is not a pedestal or Archimedean point on which one can stand for all time is not demoralizing – quite the contrary (Gigerenzer & Selten, 2001; Kahneman, Slovic, & Tversky, 1982; Kahneman & Tversky, 1973; Simon, 1962, 1982). Advances are made by self-correction; explanations evolve, get better, or are discarded (Kitcher, 1993). It is something John Dewey (1916) well appreciated at the beginning of the 20th century in his books on the logic of reasoning (Baron, 1985). Dewey (1925/1989) always appreciated that the experience of the knower was essentially embodied in information-processing systems (Schneider, 1946, 1963; Flower & Murphy, 1977; Godfrey-Smith, 1996; Kuklick, 2001; Smith, 1970, 1985; Shook, 2003). Decision analysis is a just a form of hard work; it can be done well, badly, or not at all.

The limits of rational decision making will always mandate the search for better methods. We will always have to safeguard against the disregard of contrary data, the overexaggeration of what confirms our hypothesis (Baron, 1988/2008; Popper, 1962/1971). In the end, a sense of humility and courage is always a prerequisite for claims about knowledge and decision making. Our age is one in which we hope to preserve reason without overexaggerated rationalism (Blackbun, 1998; Neville, 1992; Toulmin, 2001). Knowledge needs to be placed in a social context (e.g., Goldman, 1999; Sabini & Schulkin, 1994). The search for truth and for the value in it is the sense of humility. The experimentalist understands that hypotheses are rejected regularly – and what binds us regularly are the practices and rituals of everyday life that we wish to understand in order to evolve toward better ways of being in the world.

WATCHING AND LEARNING FROM OTHERS: COGNITIVE AND NEURAL SYSTEMS, LANGUAGE, AND ACTION. Underlying our diverse cognitive abilities is a brain with a long gestational developmental trajectory. What emerges is a cognitive predilection that includes self-corrective inquiry and trial-and-error learning, amid lots of other less noble competing motivations. A normative goal for embodied cognitive systems is to search for human scales (demythologized reason) while not abandoning our predilection for theory making, to provide and foster contexts of insight, and to improve our relationships with one another.

Diverse senses of embodied cognitive systems are inherent in the organization of action (Barsalou, 2003; Wilson, 2002). Our cognitive evolution, with its extra premium on memory and language, implodes our cognitive capabilities; our cultural evolution draws on all resources, as our memory and communicative systems are both internal and external to us (Clark, 1997; Donald, 1991). With the onset of symbolic extended and external memory in human evolution, our universe expanded exponentially.

Moreover, common regions of the brain that underlie the syntactic features of language production and comprehension (e.g., frontal cortex and basal ganglia; Ullman, 2001, 2004) also underlie diverse forms of cognitive events, including statistical reasoning and various forms of emotional informational processing. These areas are linked to action, but there is no separation from cognitive systems (Barton, 2006; Jackson & Decety, 2004; Schulkin, 2004, 2007a). Although many regions of the brain underlie the animate-inanimate distinction, a word's depiction of an action (e.g., viewing a hammer) is more likely to activate motor and premotor areas of the cortex (see, e.g., Caramazza & Mahon, 2005; Martin & Caramazza, 2003). The imagery of action – watching others, getting anchored to a world in which perception and action – are linked in fundamental ways (Jackson & Decety, 2004). Importantly, looking at action words (Hauk, Johnsrude, & Pulvermuller, 2004; Pulvermuller, Sytyrov, & Ilmoniemi, 2005), and the performance of an action activate many of the same regions of the brain (e.g., Perani et al., 1995; Martin, Ungerleider, & Haxby, 2000). The coherence in the organization of the brain is the tight link between cognitive systems and action and function (see Figure C.3).

The sense of agency and the attribution of agency to another person is something that our brain comes prepared to do (Ferrer & Frith, 2002). It underlies our sense of causal efficacy (Whitehead, 1927/1953) that is replete with the feeling of causation, of generating and moving something (James, 1890/1917). In part, this sense of causation is passive. Imitating others is represented in many different regions of the

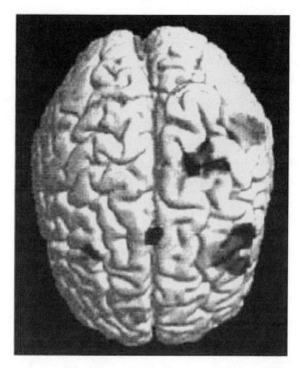

FIGURE C.3. Areas of the brain when looking at action words (Hauk et al., 2004).

brain that reflect representations of action, of motion, of agency (Chaminade, Meltzoff, & Decety, 2005). Representations of action words and regions of the brain that underlie action, and category-specific prepared knowledge about objects linked to action, show that cognitive systems traverse most if not all regions of the brain (Jackson & Decety, 2004; Schulkin, 2004). Importantly, these areas of the brain underlie the adaptation of shared experience, a sense of community (Dewey, 1934; Flanagan, 2007) and meaning (Jaspers, 1913/1997).

SELF-CORRECTIVE INQUIRY: A BRIDGE TOWARD SANITY. Embodied cognitive systems are expressed in our human experience (e.g., Clark, 1999; Gallagher, 2005; Lakoff & Johnson, 1999; Varela, Thompson, &

Rosch, 1991; Wheeler, 2005), and they underlie a multitude of forms of practice across human symbolic expression (Bourdieu, 1980/1990). What underlies those, in turn, are rich information-processing systems in the brain, now being studied in some depth (Gazzaniga, 1995/2000) and always embodied in human knowing (Changeux, 2002). A rich evolutionary background sets the conditions for human cognition (Gardenfors, 2003; Sterelny, 2004) and shapes the science that takes place (Carruthers, Stitch, & Siegal, 2002).

Still, with an eye to the past and the organization of the mind/brain (Gazzaniga, 1998) and our cultural expressions, advances in inquiry need to be linked to our existential fate (Moreno, 2003); we are great information-processing systems who have now uncovered great depths of scientific understanding. But we are obviously more than information-processing systems; we are more than the methods of our age. A variety of forms of human reasoning mark us, but two stand out: our orientation toward method and our orientation toward synthesis and ideas, what Whitehead (1929/1958) called the way of Ulysses versus Plato. Both are essential; one has been traditionally linked to the sciences and the other to the humanities. In fact, this is misleading, for both the sciences and the humanities embody both of them. The distinction is real but cuts across disciplines, just as perception, readiness, and traditions of practice are inherent in all disciplines of inquiry.

Inquiry, to be truly inquiring, must be open; people in all disciplines must be ready to appreciate the frail pursuit of truth. Truth is not easy even under the best of conditions. Reason, and its evolution as a normative goal, is to render life more meaningful; it is to live well, not as gluttons but as humbled investigators and appreciators of this wondrous life. But within life are endless hardships. Some have greater access to Fortuna than others; stoic sensibility is a necessity to own one's fate, demanding and inching out morsels of worth bit by bit. Reason helps us to imagine those great possibilities: the poet, the artist, the historian, and the scientist provide glimpses of wonder. They provide us with the teleological underpinnings of imaging, our musings, and our abduction: moments set in the context of the meaning of life.

A self-corrective conception of investigation and invention cuts across the broad range of human inquiry but needs to be anchored in historical and existential recognition of the frail sense of our human achievements with regard to the treatment of one another. With an eye toward the anti-intellectual tendencies of the dominance of method at the expense of ideas, the abject denial of self-reflection, the discarding of historical, demythologized reason reaches for the next glimmer of possibility in enriching human experience. As one noted scholar suggested, "Pragmatism was designed to make it harder for people to be driven to violence by their beliefs" (Menand, 2001). At least, that is the normative hope reflected by Emily Dickinson (1960): "Hope is the thing with feathers / That perches in the soul."

REFERENCES

Abrous, D. N., Koehl, M., & Le Moal, M. (2005). Adult neurogenesis: From precursors to network and physiology. *Physiological Reviews, 85,* 523–569.

Adolphs, R. (1999). Social cognition and the human brain. *Trends in Cognitive Sciences, 3,* 469–479.

Adolphs, R., Denburg, N. L., & Tranel, D. (2001). The amygdala's role in long-term declarative memory for gist and detail. *Behavioral Neuroscience, 112,* 983–992.

Adolphs, R., & Spezio, M. (2006). Role of the amygdala in processing visual social stimuli. *Progress in Brain Research, 156,* 363–378.

Aggleton, J. (1992/2000). *The amygdala.* Oxford: Oxford University Press.

Aiello, L. C., & Dunbar, R. I. B. (1993). Neocortex size, group size and the evolution of language. *Current Anthropology, 34,* 184–192.

Allison, T. (2001). Neuroscience and morality. *Neuroscientist, 7,* 360–364.

Alloway, T. P., Corley, M., & Ramscar, M. (2006). Seeing ahead: Experience and language in spatial perspective. *Memory and Cognition, 34,* 38–86.

Altman, J. (1966). Autoradiographic and histological studies of postnatal neurogenesis. *Journal of Comparative Neurology, 124,* 431–474.

Amaral, D. G., Bauman, M. D., & Schumann, C. M. (2003). The amygdala and autism: Implication from non-human primate studies. *Genes, Brain and Behavior, 2,* 295–302.

Anderson, D. (1997). *The radical enlightenment of Benjamin Franklin.* Baltimore: Johns Hopkins University Press.

Anderson, J. R. (1990). *The adaptive character of thought.* Hillsdale, NJ: Lawrence Erlbaum Associates.

Aristotle. (1962). *The Nicomachean ethics.* New York: Macmillan.

Aristotle. (1968). *De anima.* Oxford: Oxford University Press.

Ashwin, C., Baron-Cohen, S., Wheelwright, S., O'Riordan, M., & Bullmore, E. T. (2007). Differential activation of the amygdala and the social brain during fearful face-processing in Asperger syndrome. *Neuropsychologia, 45,* 2–14.

Atran, S. (1990/1996). *Cognitive foundations of natural history.* New York: Cambridge University Press.

Atran, S. (2002). *In gods we trust.* Oxford: Oxford University Press.

Atran, S., & Medin, D. (2008). *The native mind and the cultural construction of nature.* Boston, MA: MIT Press.

Atran, A., Medin, D. L., & Ross, N. O. (2005). The cultural mind. *Psychological Review, 112,* 744–766.

Atran, S., Medin, D., Ross, N., Lynch, E., Coley, J., Ucan Ek, E., & Vapnarsky, V. (1999). Folkecology and commons management in the Maya lowlands. *Proceedings of the National Academy of Sciences, 96,* 7598–7603.

Atran, S., & Norenzayan, A. (2004). Religion's evolutionary landscape. *Behavioral Brain Sciences, 27,* 713–770.

Augustine. (1949). *The confessions* (E. B. Pusey, Trans.). New York: Random House.

Austin, J. H. (2006). *Zen-brain reflections.* Boston, MA: MIT Press.

Bachofen, J. J. (1926/1967). *Myth, religion and Mother Right: Selected writings of J. J. Bachofen* (R. Manheim, Trans.). Princeton, NJ: Princeton University Press.

Bacon, F. (1605/1974). *The advancement of learning.* Oxford: Oxford University Press.

Baddley, A., Conway, M., & Aggleton, J. (2002). *Episodic memory.* Oxford: Oxford University Press.

Bandura, A. (2006). Toward a psychology of human agency. *Perspectives on Psychological Science, 1,* 164–180.

Barkow, J. H., Cosmides, L., & Tooby, J. (1992). *The adapted mind.* Oxford: Oxford University Press.

Baron, J. (1985). *Rationality and intelligence.* Cambridge: Cambridge University Press.

Baron, J. (1988/2008). *Thinking and deciding.* Cambridge: Cambridge University Press.

Baron-Cohen, S. (1995/2000). *Mindblindness.* Cambridge, MA: MIT Press.

Baron-Cohen, S. (2008). Autism, hypersystemizing, and truth. *Quarterly Journal of Experimental Psychology, 61,* 64–75.

Baron-Cohen, S., Knickmeyer, R. C., & Belmonte, M. K. (2005). Sex differences in the brain: Implications for explaining autism. *Science, 310,* 819–822.

Baron-Cohen, S., Ring, H. A., Bullmore, E. T., Wheelwright, S., Ashwin, C., & Williams, S. C. R. (2000). The amygdala theory of autism. *Neuroscience and Biobehavioral Review, 24,* 355–364.

Baron-Cohen, S., Ring, H. A., Wheelwright, S., Bullmore, E. T., Brammer, M. J., Simmons, A., & Williams, S. C. R. (1999). Social intelligence in the normal and autistic brain: An fMRI study. *European Journal of Neuroscience, 11,* 1–8.

Baron-Cohen, S., Tager-Flushberg, H., & Cohen, D. J. (1993/2000). *Understanding other minds.* Oxford: Oxford University Press.

Barrett, J. L. (2000). Exploring the natural foundations of religion. *Trends in Cognitive Sciences, 4,* 29–33.

Barrett, J. L., & Keil, F. C. (1996). Conceptualizing a non-natural entity: Anthropomorphism in God concepts. *Cognitive Psychology, 31,* 219–247.

Barsalou, L. W. (1999). Perceptual symbol systems. *Behavioral and Brain Sciences, 22,* 577–660.

Barsalou, L. W. (2003). Abstraction in perceptual symbol systems. *Philosophical Transactions of the Royal Society B, 358,* 1177–1187.

Barsalou, L. W. (2008). Grounded cognition. *Annual Review of Psychology, 59,* 617–645.

Barsalou, L. W., Barbey, A. K., Simmons, W. K., & Satos, A. (2005). Embodiment in religious knowledge. *Journal of Cognition and Culture, 5,* 14–57.

Barton, R. A. (2004). Binocularity and brain evolution in primates. *Proceedings of the National Academy of Sciences, 101,* 10113–10115.

Barton, R. A. (2006). Primate brain evolution: Integrating comparative neurophysiological and ethological data. *Evolutionary Anthropology, 15,* 224–236.

Bartsch, K., & Wellman, H. M. (1995). *Children's talk about the mind.* Oxford: Oxford University Press.

Barzun, J. (1989). *The culture we deserve.* Middletown, CT: Wesleyan University Press.

Bergson, H. (1908/1991). *Matter and memory.* New York: Zone Books.

Bergson, H. (1919/1946). *The creative mind* (M. Andison, Trans.). New York: Citadel Press.

Berlin, I. (1976). *Vico and Herder.* New York: Vintage Press.

Berlin, I. (1991). *The crooked timer of humanity.* New York: Knopf.

Bernard, C. (1865/1957). *An introduction to the study of experimental medicine.* New York: Dover Press.

Berridge, K. C. (2007). The debate over dopamine's role in reward: The case for incentive salience. *Physiology and Behavior, 191,* 391–431.

Berridge, K. C., & Robinson, T. E. (1998). What is the role of dopamine in reward: Hedonic impact, reward learning, or incentive salience? *Brain Research Reviews, 28,* 309–369.

Berthoz, A. (2000). *The brain's sense of movement.* Cambridge, MA: Harvard University Press.

Bird-David, N. (1999). Animism revisited. *Current Anthropology, 40,* 567–591.

Black, J. E., Issacs, K. R., Anderson, B. J., Alcantara, A. A., & Greenough, W. T. (1990). Learning causes synaptogenesis, whereas motor activity causes angiogenesis, in cerebellar cortex of adult rats. *Proceedings of the National Academy of Sciences, 87,* 5568–5572.

Blackbun, S. (1998). *Ruling passion.* Oxford, England: Clarendon.

Blakemore, S. J., Boyer, P., Pachot-Clouard, M., Meltzoff, A., Segebarth, C., & Decety, J. (2003). The detection of contingency and animacy from simple animations in the brain. *Cerebral Cortex, 13,* 837–844.

Blakemore, S. J., & Decety, J. (2001). From the perception of action to the understanding of intention. *Nature Reviews, 2,* 561–567.

Bloch, M. (1953). *The historian's craft.* New York: Knopf.

Bloom, P. (2007). Religion is natural. *Developmental Science, 10,* 147–151.

Boroditsky, L. (2000). Metaphoric structuring: Understanding time through spatial metaphors. *Cognition, 75,* 1–28.

Boroditsky, L., & Ramscar M. (2002). The roles of body and mind in abstract thought. *Psychological Science, 13,* 185–189.

Bourdieu, P. (1980/1990). *The logic of practice.* Palo Alto, CA: Stanford University Press.

Boyd, R., & Richerson, P. (1985). *Culture and evolutionary process.* Chicago: University of Chicago Press.

Boyer, P. (1990). *Tradition as truth and communication.* Cambridge: Cambridge University Press.

Boyer, P. (1994). *The naturalness of religious idea: A cognitive theory of religion.* Berkeley: University of California Press.

Boyer, P. (2001). *Religion explained.* New York: Basic Books.

Boyer, P. (2002). Religious thought and behavior as by-products of brain function. *Trends in Cognitive Science, 7,* 119–124.

Boyer, P., & Ramble, C. (2001). Cognitive templates for religious concepts: Cross-cultural evidence for recall of counter-intuitive representations. *Cognitive Science, 25,* 535–564.

Brehier, E. (1931/1965). *The Helenistic and Roman age.* Chicago: University of Chicago Press.

Brook, A., & Akins, K. (Eds.). (2005). *Cognition and the brain.* Cambridge: Cambridge University Press.

Buber, M. (1937/1970). *I and thou.* New York: Harper & Row.

Buffon, G.-L. (1749–67). *Histoire naturelle générale et particulière* (Vols. 1–15). Paris: Imprimerie Royale.

Bunning, E. (1963). *Die Physiologische Uhr,* 2nd ed. Berlin: Springer.

Burckhardt, J. (1929/1958). *The civilization of the Renaissance in Italy.* New York: Colophon Books.

Burkhardt, R. W. (1977/1995). *Lamarck and evolutionary biology.* Cambridge, MA: Harvard University Press.

Bury, J. B. (1933/1960). *The idea of progress.* New York: Dover Press.

Butterfield, H. (1981). *The origins of history.* New York: Basic Books.

Buzsaki, G. (2006). *Rhythms of the brain.* Oxford: Oxford University Press.

Byrne, R. W. (1995). *The thinking ape: Evolutionary origins of intelligence.* Oxford: Oxford University Press.

Byrne, R. W., & Corp, N. (2004). Neocortex size predicts deception rate in primates. *Proceedings of the Royal Society, 271,* 1693–1699.

Cajal, S. R. Y. (1897/1999). *Advice for a young investigator.* Cambridge, MA: MIT Press.

Cangelosi, A., & Riga, T. (2006). An embodied model for sensorimotor grounding and grounding transfer: Experiments with epigenetic robots. *Cognitive Science, 30,* 673–689.

Cannon, W. B. (1932/1963). *The wisdom of the body.* New York: W. W. Norton.

Cannon, W. B. (1945). *The way of an investigator.* New York: W. W. Norton.

Caramazza, A., & Mahon, B. Z. (2005). The organization of conceptual knowledge in the brain: The future's past and some future directions. *Cognitive Neuropsychology, 22,* 1–25.

Caramazza, A., & Shelton, J. R. (1998). Domain specific knowledge systems in the brain. *Journal of Cognitive Science, 10,* 1–34.

Carey, S. (1985/1987). *Conceptual change in childhood.* Cambridge, MA: MIT Press.

Carey, S. (2001). Cognitive foundations of arithmetic: Evolution and ontogenesis. *Mind and Language, 16,* 37–55.

Carey, S. (2003). Science education as conceptual change. *Journal of Applied Developmental Psychology, 21,* 13–19.

Carey, S. (2004). Bootstrapping and the origins of concepts. *Daedalus* (Winter), 59–68.

Carey, S., & Gelman, R. (1991). *The epigenesis of mind: Essays on biology and cognition.* Hillsdale, NJ: Lawrence Erlbaum Associates.

Carey, S., & Markman, E. M. (2000). Cognitive development. In B. M. Bly et al. (Eds.), *Cognitive science: Handbook of perception and cognition* (2d ed.). San Diego, CA: Academic Press, pp. 202–254.

Carey, S., & Smith, C. (1993). On understanding the nature of scientific knowledge. *Educational Psychologist, 28,* 235–251.

Carruthers, P., Stitch, S., & Siegal, M. (2002). *The cognitive basis of science.* Cambridge: Cambridge University Press.

Carter, C. S. (2007). Sex differences in oxytocin and vasopressin: Implications for autism spectrum disorders? *Behavioural Brain Research, 176,* 170–186.

Carter, C. S., Lederhendler, I. L., & Kirkpatrick, B. (1997/1999). *The integrative neurobiology of affiliation.* Cambridge, MA: MIT Press.

Casasanto, D., & Boroditsky, L. (2008). Time in the mind: Using space to think about time. *Cognition, 106,* 579–593.

Casebeer, W. D. (2003). *Natural ethical facts.* Cambridge, MA: MIT Press.

Cassirer, E. (1944/1978). *An essay on man.* New Haven, CT: Yale University Press.

Cassirer, E. (1946). *Language and myth.* New York: Harper & Row.

Cassirer, E. (1953/1957). *Philosophy of symbolic forms* (Vols. 1–3). New Haven, CT: Yale University Press.

Castelli, F., Happe, F., Frith, U., & Frith, C. (2000). Movement and mind: A functional imaging study of perception and interpretation of complex intentional movement patterns. *Neuroimage, 12,* 314–325.

Chaminade, T., Meltzoff, A. N., & Decety, J. (2002). Does the end justify the means? A PET exploration of the mechanisms involved in human imitation. *Neuroimage, 15,* 318–328.

Chan, W. J. (1963). *A source book in Chinese philosophy.* Princeton, NJ: Princeton University Press.

Changeux, J. P. (2002). *The physiology of truth.* Cambridge, MA: Harvard University Press.

Cheney, D. L., & Seyfarth, R. M. (1990). *How monkeys see the world.* Chicago: University of Chicago Press.

Cheney, D. L., & Seyfarth, R. M. (2007). *Baboon metaphysics.* Chicago: University of Chicago Press.

Cherniak, C. (1986). *Minimal rationality.* Cambridge, MA: MIT Press.

Chomsky, N. (1965). *Aspects of the theory of syntax.* Cambridge, MA: MIT Press.

Chomsky, N. (1972). *Language and mind.* New York: Harcourt Brace Jovanovich.

Clark, A. (1997). *Being there.* Cambridge, MA: MIT Press.

Clark, A. (1999). An embodied cognitive science? *Trends in Cognitive Sciences, 3,* 345–351.

Clark, A. (2003). *Natural-born cyborgs.* Oxford: Oxford University Press.

Clark, W. (2006). *Academic charisma and the origins of the research university.* Chicago: University of Chicago Press.

Comery, T. A., Stamoudis, C. X., Irwin, S. A., & Greenough, W. T. (1996). Increased density of multiple-head dendritic spines on medium-sized spiny neurons of the striatum in rats reared in a complex environment. *Neurobiology of Learning and Memory, 66,* 93–96.

Cohen, M. R. (1931/1959). *Reason and nature.* New York: Dover Press.

Collingwood, R. G. (1929/1978). *An autobiography.* Oxford: Oxford University Press.

Collingwood, R. G. (1945/1976). *The idea of nature.* Oxford: Oxford University Press.

Collingwood, R. G. (1946/1956). *The idea of history.* Oxford: Oxford University Press.

Collingwood, R. G. (2001). *The principles of history* (W. H. Dray & W. J. Van Der Dussen, Eds.). Oxford: Oxford University Press.

Comte, A. C. (1842/1975). *A general view of positivism* (J. Bridges, Trans.). New York: Robert Speller & Sons.

Conze, E. (1951/1975). *Buddhism: Its essence and development.* New York: Harper & Row.

Conze, E. (1959/1984). *Buddhistic scriptures.* New York: Penguin Books.

Corballis, M. C. (2002). *From hand to mouth.* Princeton, NJ: Princeton University Press.

Corballis, M. C., & Lea, S. E. G. (Eds.). (1999). *The descent of mind.* New York: Oxford University Press.

Craig, W. (1918). Appetites and aversions as constituents of instinct. *Biological Bulletin, 34,* 91–107.

Critchley, H. D. (2005). Neural mechanisms of autonomic, affective, and cognitive integration. *Journal of Comparative Neurology, 493,* 154–166.

Critchley, H. D., Daly, E. M., Bullmore, E. T., Williams, S. C. R., Van Amelsvoort, T., Robertson, D. M., et al. (2000). The functional neuroanatomy of social behaviour: Changes in cerebral blood flow when people with autistic disorder process facial expressions. *Brain, 123,* 2203–2212.

Critchley, H. D., Mathias, C. J., Josephs, O., O'Doherty, J., Zanini, S., Dewar, B. K., et al. (2003). Human cingulate cortex and autonomic control: Converging neuroimaging and clinical evidence. *Brain, 126,* 2139–2152.

Croce, B. (1941). *History as the story of liberty.* Chicago: Henry Regnery Co.

Dallman, M. F. (2007). Modulation of stress responses: How we cope with excess glucocorticoids. *Experimental Neurology, 206,* 179–182.

Damasio, A. R. (1996). The somatic marker hypothesis and the possible functions of the prefrontal cortex. *Philosophical Transactions of the Royal Society, 351,* 1413–1420.

Damasio, A. R. (1999). *The feeling of what happens.* New York: Harcourt.

Darwin, C. (1859/1958). *The origin of species.* New York: Mentor Books.

Darwin, C. (1871/1874). *The descent of man.* New York: Rand McNally.

Darwin, C. (1872/1965). *The expression of emotions in man and animals.* Chicago: University of Chicago Press.

Darwin, E. (1789/1991). *The book of plants: Vol. 2.* Oxford: Woodstock Books.

Darwin, E. (1794/1801). *Zoonomia, or the law of organic life* (3d ed.). London: J. Johnson.

Dasser, V., Ulbaek, I., & Premack, D. (1989). The perception of intention. *Science, 243,* 365–367.

Davidson, R. J., & Harrington, A. (2002). *Visions of compassion.* Oxford: Oxford University Press.

Davidson, R. J., Kabat-Zinn, J., Schumacher, J., Rosenkranz, B. A., Muller, M., Saki, F., et al. (2003). Alterations in brain and immune function produced by mindfulness meditation. *Psychosomatic Medicine, 65,* 564–570.

Dawkins, R. (2006). *The God delusion.* Boston: Houghton Mifflin.

Dayes, R. M. (2001). *Everyday irrationality.* Boulder, CO: Westview Press.

Deacon, T. W. (1997). *The symbolic species.* New York: W. W. Norton.

Dear, P. (1995). *Discipline and experience.* Chicago: University of Chicago Press.

Dear, P. (2006). *The intelligibility of nature.* Chicago: University of Chicago Press.

Decety, J. (1996). Do imagined and executed actions share the same neural substrate? *Cognitive Brain Research, 3,* 87–93.

Decety, J., & Jackson, P. W. (2006). A social neuroscience perspective on empathy. *Current Directions in Psychological Science, 15,* 54–58.

Decety, J., Perani, D., & Jeannerod, M. (1994). Mapping motor representations with positron emission tomography. *Nature, 371,* 600–602.

Deheane, S., Izard, V., Pica, P., & Spelke, E. (2006). Core knowledge of geometry in an Amazonian Indigene group. *Science, 311,* 381–384.

Delza, S. (1961/1985). *Tai-chi ch'uan.* Albany: State University of New York Press.

Dennett, D. (1987). *The intentional stance.* Cambridge, MA: MIT Press.

Dennett, D. (2006). *Breaking the spell.* New York: Viking Press.

Derrida, J. (1972/1981). *Dissemination.* Chicago: University of Chicago Press.

Descartes, R. (1663/1967). *Discourse on method and meditations.* Indianapolis: Bobbs-Mettill Co.

De Waal, F. B. M. (2000). Primates: A natural heritage of conflict resolution. *Science, 289,* 586–590.

De Waal, F., & Lanting, F. (1997). *Bonobo: The forgotten ape.* Berkeley: University of California Press.

Dewey, J. (1896). The reflex arc concept in psychology. *Psychological Review, 3,* 357–370.

Dewey, J. (1902/1974). *The child and the curriculum and the school and society.* Chicago: University of Chicago Press.

Dewey, J. (1908/1960). *Theory of moral life.* New York: Holt, Rinehart & Winston.

Dewey, J. (1909/1975). *Moral principles in education.* Carbondale: Southern Illinois University Press.

Dewey, J. (1910/1965). *The influence of Darwin on philosophy.* Bloomington: Indiana University Press.

Dewey, J. (1916). *Essays in experimental logic.* Chicago: University of Chicago Press.

Dewey, J. (1920/1948). *Reconstruction in philosophy.* Boston: Beacon Press.

Dewey, J. (1925/1989). *Experience and nature.* La Salle, IL: Open Court.

Dewey, J. (1929/1960). *The quest for certainty.* New York: Capricorn Books.

Dewey, J. (1934/1970). *A common faith.* New Haven, CT: Yale University Press.

Dewey, J. (1938). *Logic: The theory of inquiry.* New York: Henry Holt and Co., Inc.

Dewey, J. (1938/1972). *Experience and education.* New York: Collier-MacMillan.

Dickinson, E. (1960). *Selected poems.* New York: Dell.

Dilthey, W. (1926/1961). *Pattern and meaning in history* (H. Richman, Trans.). New York: HarperTorch.

di Pellegrino, G., Fadiga, L., Fogassi, L., Gallese, V., & Rizzolatti, G. (1992). Understanding motor events: A neurophysiological study. *Experimental Brain Research, 91,* 176–180.

Dobzhansky, T. C. (1962). *Mankind evolving.* New Haven, CT: Yale University Press.

Dolan, R. J. (2007). The human amygdala and orbital prefrontal cortex in behavioural regulation. *Philosophical Transactions of the Royal Society B, 362,* 787–799.

Dolgin, K. G., & Behrend, D. A. (1984). Children's knowledge about animates and inanimates. *Child Development, 35,* 1645–1650.

Donald, M. (1991). *Origins of modern man.* Cambridge, MA: Harvard University Press.

Donald, M. (2004). The virtues of rigorous interdisciplinarity. In J. M. Luraciello, J. A. Hudson, R. Fivush, & P. J. Baver (Eds.), *The development of the mediated mind.* Mahwah, NJ: Lawrence Erlbaum Associates, pp. 245–256.

Duchaine, B., Cosmides, L., & Tooby, H. (2001). Evolutionary psychology and the brain. *Current Opinion in Neurobiology, 11,* 225–250.

Dunbar, R. I. M. (1992). Neocortex size as a constraint on group size in primates. *Journal of Human Evolution, 22,* 469–493.

Dunbar, R. I. M. (1996). *Grooming, gossip and the evolution of language.* London: Faber & Faber.

Dunbar, R. I. M. (2003). The social brain. *Annual Review of Anthropology, 32,* 163–181.

Dunbar, R. I. M., & Shultz, S. (2007). Understanding primate evolution. *Philosophical Transactions of the Royal Society, 362,* 649–658.

Dupré, J. (1993). *The disorder of things.* Cambridge, MA: Harvard University Press.

Dupré, J. (2003). *Darwin's legacy.* Oxford: Oxford University Press.

Durkheim, E. (1915/1965). *The elementary forms of religious life.* New York: Free Press.

Durkheim, E. (1974). *Sociology and philosophy* (D. F. Pocock, Trans.). New York: Free Press.

Edwards, J. (1754/1969). *Freedom of the will* (A. S. Kaufman & W. K. Frankena, Eds.). New York: Bobbs-Merrill.

Eichenbaum, H., & Cohen, N. J. (2001). *From conditioning to conscious recollection.* Oxford: Oxford University Press.

Eiseley, L. (1959/1961). *Darwin's century.* New York: Anchor Books.

Ekman, P. (1972). Universals and cultural differences in facial expressions of emotion. In J. Cole (Ed.), *Nebraska symposium on motivation, 1971.* Lincoln: University of Nebraska Press, pp. 207–283.

Ekman, P., Davidson, R. J., Ricard, M., & Wallace, B. A. (2005). Buddhist and psychological perspectives on emotion and well-being. *Current Directions in Psychological Science, 14,* 59–63.

Eliade, M. (1959). *The sacred and the profane; the nature of religion.* New York: Harcourt.

Eldridge, N. (1985). *Unfinished synthesis.* Oxford: Oxford University Press.

Eldridge, N. (1999). *The pattern of evolution.* New York: W. H. Freeman.

Elster, J. (1979/1988). *Ulysses and the Sirens.* Cambridge: Cambridge University Press.

Elster, J. (1983/1988). *Explaining technical change.* Cambridge: Cambridge University Press.

Emerson, Ralph Waldo (1855/1883). *Nature, addresses and lectures.* Cambridge: Riverside Press.

Emery, N. J., & Amaral, D. G. (2000). The role of the amygdala in primate social cognition. In R. D. Lane & L. Nadel (Eds.), *Cognitive neuroscience of emotion.* New York: Oxford University Press, pp. 156–191.

Emery, N. J., Lorincz, E. N., Perrett, D. I., Oram, M. W., & Baker, C. I. (1997). Gaze following and joint attention in Rhesus monkeys (Macaca mulatta). *Journal of Comparative Psychology, 111,* 286–293.

Erickson, K., Drevets, W. C., & Schulkin, J. (2003). Glucocorticoid regulation of diverse cognitive functions in normal and pathological emotional states. *Neuroscience and Biobehavioral Reviews, 27,* 233–246.

Erickson, K., Mah, L., Schulkin, J., Charney, W. S., & Drevets, W. C. (2005). Effects of hydrocorticosterone infusion on affectively valenced autobiographical memory. *Neuroscience Abstracts.*

Fauconnier, G., & Turner, M. (2003). *The way we think.* New York: Basic Books

Fesmire, S. (2003). *John Dewey and moral imagination: Pragmatism in ethics.* Bloomington: Indiana University Press.

Finley, M. I. (1971). *The use and abuse of history.* New York: Penguin Books.

Fiorillo, C. D., Tobler, P. N., & Schultz, W. (2003). Discrete coding of reward probability and uncertainty by dopamine neurons. *Science, 299,* 1898–1902.

Fiske, A. P. (1991). *Structures of social life.* New York: Free Press.

Flanagan, O. (2007). *The really hard problems.* Cambridge, MA: MIT Press.

Fleagle, J. G. (1988). *Primate adaptation and evolution.* San Diego: Academic Press.

Flower, E., & Murphy, M. G. (1977). *A history of philosophy in America* (Vols. 1–2). New York: Capricorn Books.

Fodor, J. (1983). *The modularity of mind.* Cambridge, MA: MIT Press.

Fogassi, L., & Luppino, G. (2005). Motor functions of the parietal lobe. *Current Opinion in Neurobiology, 15,* 626–631.

Fogassi, L., Ferrari, P. F., Gesierich, B., Rozzi, S., Chersi, F., & Rizzolatti, G. (2005). Parietal lobe: From action organization to intention understanding. *Science, 308,* 662–666.

Foley, R. (1995). *Humans before humanity.* Oxford, England: Blackwell.

Foley, R. (1996). An evolutionary and chronological framework for human social behaviour. *Proceedings of the British Academy, 88,* 95–117.

Foley, R. (2001). In the shadow of the modern synthesis? *Evolutionary Anthropology, 10,* 5–14.

Foley, R., & Lahr, M. M. (2003). On stony ground: Lithic technology, human evolution and the emergence of culture. *Evolutionary Anthropology, 12,* 109–122.

Foley, R., & Lahr, M. M. (2004). Human evolution writ small. *Nature, 431,* 1043–1044.

Fonberg, E. (1974). Amygdala function within the alimentary system. *Aeta Neurobiologae Experimentalis, 22,* 51–57.

Foner, E. (2002). *Who owns history?* New York: Hill & Wang.

Foster, R. G., & Kreitzman, L. (2004). *Rhythms of life.* New Haven, CT: Yale University Press.

Franklin, B. (1726, 1757/1987). *Essays, articles, bagatelles, and letters: Poor Richard's almanac.* New York: Library Classics.

Frazer, J. H. (1921/2000). *The new golden bough.* New York: Bartleby.

Freud, S. (1924/1960). *A general introduction to psychoanalysis.* New York: Washington Square Press.

Freud, S. (1927/1964). *The future of an illusion.* New York: Doubleday.

Frith, C. D. (2007). The social brain? *Philosophical Transactions of the Royal Society B, 362*, 671–678.

Frith, C. D., & Frith, U. (1999). Interacting minds: A biological basis. *Science, 286*, 1692–1694.

Frith, C., & Wolpert, D. (2003). *The neuroscience of social interaction.* Oxford: Oxford University Press.

Fromm, E. (1947). *Man for himself.* New York: Rinehart.

Fromm, E. (1950/1972). *Psychoanalysis and religion.* New York: Doubleday.

Fromm, E., Suzuki, D. T., & De Martino, R. (1960/1970). *Zen Buddhism and psychoanalysis.* New York: Harper & Row.

Fuller, S. (1988). *Social epistemology.* Bloomington: Indiana University Press.

Gage, F. H. (1998). Stem-cells of the central nervous system. *Current Opinion in Neurobiology, 8,* 671–676.

Galileo, G. (1957). *Discoveries and opinions.* New York: Anchor Books.

Galison, P. (1988). History, philosophy and the central metaphor. *Science in Context, 3,* 197–212.

Galison, P. (1999). Objectivity is romantic. In *The Humanities and the Sciences. American Council of Learned Societies.Occasional Paper* No 47, 15–43.

Gallagher, S. (2005). *How the body shapes the mind.* Oxford: Oxford University Press.

Gallagher, S., & Meltzoff, A. N. (1996). The earliest sense of self and others: Merleau-Ponty and recent developmental studies. *Philosophical Psychology, 9,* 211–233.

Gallese, V. (2007). Before and below 'theory of mind': Embodied simulation and the neural correlates of social cognition. *Philosophical Transactions of the Royal Society B, 362,* 659–669.

Gallistel, C. R. (1990). *The organization of learning.* Cambridge, MA: MIT Press.

Gandhi, M. (1964). *On non-violence* (T. Merton, Ed.). New York: New Directions.

Gardenfors, P. (2003). *How Homo became sapiens: On the evolution of thinking.* Oxford: Oxford University Press.

Gardner, H. (1985). *The mind's new science.* New York: Basic Books.

Gazzaniga, M. S. (1995/2000). *The new cognitive neurosciences.* Cambridge, MA: MIT Press.

Gazzaniga, M. S. (1998). *The mind's past.* Berkeley: University of California Press.

Gelman, R., Durgin, F., & Kaufman, L. (1995). Distinguishing between animates and inanimates: Not by motion alone. In D. Sperber, D. Premack, & A. Premack (Eds.), *Causal cognition.* Oxford, England: Clarendon Press, pp. 150–184.

Gelman, R., Spelke, E. S., & Meck, E. (1983). What preschoolers know about animate and inanimate objects. In D. Rogers & J. A. Sloboda (Eds.), *The acquisition of symbolic skills.* New York: Plenum, pp. 297–326.

Gelman, S. A. (2003). *The essential child.* Oxford: Oxford University Press.

Gelman, S. A., & Markman, E. M. (1987). Young children's inductions from natural kinds. *Child Development, 58,* 1532–1541.

Geschwind, N. (1974). *Selected papers on language and the brain.* Boston: Reidel Publishing.

Gibbon, E. (1788/1952). *The decline and fall of the Roman Empire.* New York: Penguin Books.

Gibbs, R. W. (2006). *Embodiment and cognitive science.* Cambridge: Cambridge University Press.

Gibson, J. J. (1966). *The senses considered as perceptual systems.* New York: Houghton Mifflin.

Gibson, K. R., & Ingold, T. (Eds.). (1993). *Tools, language and cognition in human evolution.* Cambridge: Cambridge University Press.

Giere, R. N. (2006). *Scientific perspectivism.* Chicago: University of Chicago Press.

Gigerenzer, G. (2007). *Gut feelings.* New York: Viking Press.

Gigerenzer, G., & Selten, R. (2001). *Bounded rationality.* Cambridge, MA: MIT Press.

Gigerenzer, G. (2000). *Adaptive thinking: Rationality in the real world.* New York: Oxford University Press.

Glenberg, A. M. (1997). What memory is for. *Behavioral and Brain Sciences, 20,* 1–55.

Glenberg, A. M., Gutierrez, T., Levin, J. R., Japuntich, S., & Kaschak, M. P. (2004). Activity and imagined activity can enhance young children's reading comprehension. *Journal of Educational Psychology, 96,* 424–436.

Glenberg, A. M., & Kaschak, M. P. (2002). Grounding language in action. *Psychonomic Bulletin & Review, 9,* 558–565.

Gloor, P. (1997). *The temporal lobe and limbic system.* New York: Oxford University Press.

Godfrey-Smith, P. (1996). *Complexity and the function of mind.* Cambridge: Cambridge University Press.

Godfrey-Smith, P. (2002). Dewey on naturalism, realism and science. *Philosophy of Science, 69,* S1–S11.

Goffman, E. (1971). *Relations in public.* New York: Harper & Row.

Goldman, A. I. (1999). *Knowledge in a social world.* Oxford: Oxford University Press.

Goldsmith, R. (1940/1982). *The material basis of evolution.* New Haven, CT: Yale University Press.

Gopnik, A., Glymour, C., Sobel, D., Schulz, L., Kushnir, T., & Danks, D. (2004). A theory of causal learning in children: Causal maps and Bayes nets. *Psychological Review, 111,* 1–31.

Gopnik, A., & Meltzoff, A. N. (1997). *Words, thoughts and theories.* Cambridge, MA: MIT Press.

Gould, E., Beylin, A., Tanapat, P., Reeves, A., & Shors, T. J. (1999). Learning enhances adult neurogenesis in the hippocampal formation. *Nature Neuroscience, 2,* 260–265.

Gould, E., & McEwen, B. (1993). Neuronal birth and death. *Current Opinion in Neurobiology, 3,* 676–682.

Gould, E., Reeves, A. J., Craziano, M. S. A., & Gross, C. G. (1999). Neurogenesis in the neocortex of adult primates. *Science, 286,* 548–552.

Gould, E., Vall, N., Wagers, M., & Gross, C. G. (2001). Adult generated hippocampal and neocortical neurons in macaques have a transient existence. *Proceedings of the National Academy of Sciences, 98,* 10910–10916.

Gould, S. J. (1977). *Ontogeny and phylogeny.* Cambridge, MA: Harvard University Press.

Gould, S. J. (2002). *The structure of evolutionary theory.* Cambridge, MA: Harvard University Press.

Gould, S. J., & Eldridge, N. (1977). Punctuated equilibria: The tempo and mode of evolution reconsidered. *Paleobiology, 3,* 115–151.

Gould, S. J., & Lewontin, R. C. (1979). The spandrels of San Marco and the Panglossian paradigm: A critique of the adaptationist programme. *Proceedings of the Royal Society B, 205*(1161), 581–598.

Green, L., Fein, D., Modahl, C., Feinstein, C., Waterhouse, L., & Morris, M. (2001). Oxytocin and autistic disorder: Alterations in peptide forms. *Biological Psychiatry, 50,* 609–613.

Greene, J. D., Sommerville, R. B., Nystrom, L. E., Darley, J. M., & Cohen, J. D. (2001). An fMRI investigation of emotional engagement in moral judgment. *Science, 293,* 2105–2108.

Greenough, W. T., & Volkmar, F. R. (1973). Pattern of dendritic branching in occipital cortex of rats reared in complex environments. *Experimental Neurology, 40,* 491–504.

Grene, M. (1995). *A philosophical testament.* Chicago: Open Court.

Grice, P. (1957). Meaning. *The Philosophical Review, 3,* 377–388.

Guthrie, R. D. (2005). *The nature of Paleolithic art.* Chicago: University of Chicago Press.

Habermas, J. (1967/1988). *On the logic of the social sciences* (S. W. Nicholson & J. A. Stark, Trans.). Cambridge, MA: MIT Press.

Hacking, I. (1975). *The emergence of probability.* Cambridge: Cambridge University Press.

Hacking, I. (1990). *The taming of chance.* Cambridge: Cambridge University Press.

Hacking, I. (1999). *The social construction of what?* Cambridge, MA: Harvard University Press.

Haidt, J. (2006). *The happiness hypothesis: Finding modern truth in ancient wisdom.* New York: Basic Books.

Hanson, N. R. (1958/1972). *Patterns of discovery.* Cambridge: Cambridge University Press.

Hari, R., Forss, N., Avikainen, S., Kirverskari, E., Salenius, S., & Rizzolatti, G. (1998). Activation of human primary cortex during action observation: A neuromagnetic study. *Proceedings of the National Academy of Sciences, 95,* 15061–15065.

Harrington, A., & Zajonc, A. (2006). *The Dalai Lama.* Cambridge, MA: MIT Press.

Harvey, W. (1651/1965). *Anatomical exercises on the generation of animals.* New York: Johnson Reprint Corp.

Haskell, T. L. (1998). *Objectivity is not neutrality.* Baltimore: Johns Hopkins University Press.

Haskins, C. H. (1923/1957). *The rise of the universities.* Ithaca, NY: Cornell University Press.

Hauk, O., Johnsrude, I., & Pulvermuller, F. (2004). Somatotopic representation of action words in human motor and premotor cortex. *Neuron, 41,* 301–307.

Hauser, M. D. (2000). *Wild minds.* New York: Henry Holt.

Hauser, M. D., Chomsky, N., & Fitch, W. T. (2002). The faculty of language: What is it, who has it and how did it evolve? *Science, 298,* 1569–1579.

Heelan, P. A. (1983). *Space perception and the philosophy of science.* Berkeley: University of California Press.

Heelan, P. A. (1994). *Galileo, Luther, and the hermeneutics of natural science: The question of hermeneutics* (T. J. Stapleton, Ed.). Netherlands: Kluwer Academic Publishers.

Heelan, P. A., & Schulkin, J. (1998). Hermeneutical philosophy and pragmatism: A philosophy of the science. *Synthese, 115,* 269–302.

Heidegger, M. (1927/1962). *Being and time* (J. Macquarrie & E. Robinson, Trans.). New York: Harper & Row.

Hendel, C. W. (1959). *John Dewey and the experimental spirit in philosophy.* New Haven, CT: Yale University Press.

Herbert, J., & Schulkin, J. (2002). Neurochemical coding of adaptive responses in the limbic system. In D. Pfaff (Ed.), *Hormones, brain and behavior.* New York: Elsevier, pp. 659–689.

Herodotus (1954). *The histories* (A. de Selincourt, Trans.). Baltimore: Penguin Books.

Himmelfarb, G. (1959/1962). *Darwin and the Darwinian revolution.* New York: W. W. Norton.

Hirschfield, L. A., & Gelman, S. A. (1994). *Mapping the mind.* Cambridge: Cambridge University Press.

Hirshman, A. O. (1982). *Shifting involvements.* Princeton, NJ: Princeton University Press.

Hollander, E., Bartz, J., Chaplin, W., Phillips, A., Sumner, J., Soorya, L., et al. (2006). Oxytocin increases retention of social cognition in autism. *Biological Psychiatry, 61,* 498–503.

Hollander, E., Novotny, S., Hanratty, M., Yaffe, R., DeCaria, C. M., Aronowitz, B. R., et al. (2003). Oxytocin infusion reduces repetitive behaviors in adults with autistic and Asperger's disorders. *Neuropsychopharmacology, 28,* 193–198.

Houser, N., Eller, J. R., Lewis, A. C., De Tienne, A., Clark, C. L., & Bront Davis, D. (1998). *The essential Peirce: Vol. 2 (1893–1913).* Bloomington: Indiana University Press.

Houser, N., & Kloesel, C. (1992/1998). *The essential Peirce: Vol. 1 (1867–1893).* Bloomington: Indiana University Press.

Houser, N., Roberts, D. D., & Van Evra, J. (Eds.). (1997). *Studies in the logic of Charles Sanders Peirce.* Indianapolis: University of Indiana Press.

Howells, W. (1963). *Back of history.* New York: Anchor Books.

Hull, D. L. (1988). *Science as a process.* Chicago: University of Chicago Press.

Humbolt, W. V. (1836/1971). *Linguistic and intellectual development.* Philadelphia: University of Pennsylvania Press.

Hume, D. (1757/1957). *The natural history of religion.* Stanford, CA: Stanford University Press.

Humphrey, N. (1976). The social function of intellect. In P. P. G. Bateson & R. A. Hinde (Eds.), *Growing points in ethology.* Cambridge: Cambridge University Press, pp. 307–317.

Humphrey, N. (2000). Cave art, autism and the human mind. *Journal of Consciousness Studies, 6,* 116–123.

Huxley, T. H. (1863). *Man's place in nature.* London: Macmillan.

Huxley, T. H. (1909). *Autobiography and selected essays.* Cambridge, MA: Houghton Mifflin.

Iacoboni, M. (2005). Neural mechanisms of imitation. *Current Opinions in Neurobiology, 15*(6), 632–637.

Iacoboni, M., Lieberman, M. D., Knowlton, B. J., Molnar-Szakacs, I., Moritz, M., Throop, J., & Fiske, A. P. (2004). Watching social interactions produces dorsomedial prefrontal and medial parietal BOLD fMRI signal increases compared to a resting baseline. *NeuroImage, 21*, 1167–1173.

Iacoboni, M., Woods, R. P., Brass, M., Bekkering, H., Mazziotta, J. C., & Rizzolatti, G. (1999). Cortical mechanisms of imitation. *Science, 286*, 2526–2528.

Insel, T. R., & Fernald, R. D. (2004). How the brain processes social information. *Annual Review of Neuroscience, 27*, 697–722.

Insel, T. R., O'Brien, D. J., & Leckman, J. F. (1999). Oxytocin, vasopressin, and autism: Is there a connection? *Biological Psychiatry, 45*, 145–157.

Israel, J. I. (2001). *Radical enlightenment.* Oxford: Oxford University Press.

Jackendoff, R. (1992). *Language of the mind.* Cambridge, MA: MIT Press.

Jackson, J. H. (1884/1958). Evolution and dissolution of the nervous system. In J. Taylor (Ed.), *Collected works of John Hughlings Jackson: Vol. 11.* London: Staples Press, pp. 45–118.

Jackson, P. L., & Decety, J. (2004). Motor cognition. *Current Opinion in Neurobiology, 14*, 259–263.

Jacob, P., & Jeannerod, M. (2003). *Ways of seeing.* Oxford: Oxford University Press.

Jacob, P., & Jeannerod, M. (2005). The motor theory of social cognition: A critique. *Trends in Cognitive Science, 9*, 21–25.

James, W. (1887). Some human instincts. *Popular Science Monthly, 31*, 160–176.

James, W. (1890/1917). *Principles of psychology.* New York: Henry Holt.

James, W. (1896/1956). *The will to believe, human immortality.* New York: Dover Press.

James, W. (1902/1974). *The varieties of religious experience: A study in human nature.* New York: Collier Books, Macmillan.

James, W. (1910/1970). *Pragmatism and other essays.* New York: Washington Square Press.

Jaspers, K. (1913/1997). *General psychopathology.* Baltimore: Johns Hopkins University Press.

Jaspers, K. (1949/1968). *The origin and goal of history* (M. Bullock, Trans.). New Haven, CT: Yale University.

Jaspers, K. (1951/1954). *Way to wisdom.* New Haven, CT: Yale University Press.

Jeannerod, M. (1999). To act or not to act: Perspectives on the representation of action. *Quarterly Journal of Experimental Psychology, 52*, 1–29.

Jevning, R., Wilson, A. F., & VanderLaan, E. F. (1978). Plasma prolactin and growth hormone during meditation. *Psychosomatic Medicine, 40*, 329–333.

Johanson, D. C., & Edey, M. (1981). *Lucy: The beginnings of humankind.* New York: Simon & Schuster.

Johnson, M. (1987/1990). *The body in the mind.* Chicago: University of Chicago Press.

Johnson, M. (1993). *Moral imagination.* Chicago: University of Chicago Press.

Johnson, M. (2007). *The meaning of the body.* Chicago: University of Chicago Press.

Johnson, M., & Rohrer, T. (2007). We are live creatures: Embodiment, American pragmatism and the cognitive organism. In *Body, language and mind: Vol. 1.* Berlin: Mouton de Gruyter, pp. 17–54.

Johnson-Laird, P. N. (2001). Mental models and deduction. *Trends in Cognitive Science, 5,* 434–442.

Johnson-Laird, P. N. (2002). Peirce, logic diagrams, and the elementary operations of reasoning. *Thinking and Reasoning, 8,* 69–95.

Jolly, A. (1966). Lemur social behavior and primate intelligence. *Science, 153,* 501–506.

Jolly, A. (1999). *Lucy's legacy.* Cambridge, MA: Harvard University Press.

Kagan, J. (1984). *The nature of the child.* New York: Basic Books.

Kagan, J. (2002). *Surprise, uncertainty and mental structure.* Cambridge, MA: Harvard University Press.

Kahneman, D., Slovic, P., & Tversky, A. (Eds.). (1982). *Judgment under uncertainty: Heuristics and biases.* New York: Cambridge University Press.

Kahneman, D., & Tversky, A. (1973). On the psychology of prediction. *Psychological Review, 80,* 237–251.

Kant, I. (1787/1965). *Critique of pure reason* (L. W. Beck, Trans.). New York: St. Martin's Press.

Kant, I. (1788/1956). *Critique of practical reason* (L. W. Beck, Trans.). New York: Bobbs-Merrill.

Kant, I. (1792/1951). *Critique of judgment.* New York: Hafner Press.

Keil, F. (1979). *Semantic and conceptual development: An ontological perspective.* Cambridge, MA: Harvard University Press.

Keil, F. (1983). On the emergence of semantic and conceptual distinctions. *Journal of Experimental Psychology, 112,* 357–385.

Keil, F. C. (2007). Biology and beyond: Domain specificity in a broader developmental context. *Human Development, 50,* 31–38.

Keil, F. C., & Wilson, R. A. (2000). *Explanation and cognition.* Cambridge, MA: MIT Press.

Kelley, A. E. (1999). Neural integrative activities of nucleus accumbens subregions in relation to learning and motivation. *Psychobiology, 27,* 198–213.

Keltner, D., & Haidt, J. (2003). Approaching awe, a moral, spiritual, and aesthetic emotion. *Cognition and Emotion, 17,* 297–314.

Kempermann, G. (2006). *Adult neurogenesis.* Oxford: Oxford University Press.

Kempermann, G., Kuhn, H. G., & Gage, F. H. (1999). Experience-induced neurogenesis in the senescent dentate gyrus. *Journal of Neuroscience, 18,* 3206–3212.

Kempermann, G., Wiskott, L., & Gage, F. H. (2004). Functional significance of adult neurogenesis. *Current Opinion in Neurobiology, 14,* 186–191.

Kierkegaard, S. (1844/1980). *Fear and trembling and the sickness unto death.* Princeton, NJ: Princeton University Press.

King, B. J. (2007). *Evolving God.* New York: Doubleday.

King-Hele, D. (1986). *Erasmus Darwin and the romantic poets.* New York: Macmillan.

Kirk, G. S., & Raven, J. E. (1957). *The presocratic philosophers.* Cambridge: Cambridge University Press.

Kitcher, P. (1990). *Kant's transcendental psychology.* Oxford: Oxford University Press.

Kitcher, P. (1993). *The advancement of science.* Oxford: Oxford University Press.

Kitcher, P. (1996). *The lives to come.* New York: Simon & Schuster.

Kitcher, P. (2007). *Living with Darwin.* Oxford: Oxford University Press.

Klintsova, A. Y., & Greenough, W. T. (1999). Synaptic plasticity in cortical systems. *Current Opinion in Neurobiology, 9,* 203–208.

Knowlton, B., Mangels, J., & Squire, L. (1996). A neostriatal habit learning system in humans. *Science, 273,* 1399–1402.

Kornblith, H. (1993). *Inductive inference and its natural ground.* Cambridge, MA: MIT Press.

Kosslyn, S. M., Alpert, N. M., & Thompson, W. L. (1993). Visual mental imagery and visual perception: PET studies. In *Functional MRI of the brain.* Arlington, VA: Society for Magnetic Resonance Imaging, pp. 183–190.

Koyre, A. (1961). *Renaissance thought: The classic, scholastic, and humanist strains.* New York: HarperTorch.

Koyre, A. (1968). *Metaphysics and measurement: Essays in scientific revolution.* Cambridge, MA: Harvard University Press.

Kripke, S. (1980). *Naming and necessity.* Cambridge, MA: Harvard University Press.

Krieckhaus, E. E. (1970). Innate recognition aids rats in sodium regulation. *Journal of Comparative and Physiological Psychology, 73,* 117–122.

Krieckhaus, E. E., & Wolf, G. (1968). Interaction of innate mechanisms and latent learning. *Journal of Comparative and Physiological Psychology, 65,* 197–201.

Kuhn, T. S. (1962). *The structure of scientific revolution.* Chicago: University of Chicago Press.

Kuhn, T. S. (1971). The relations between history and the history of science. *Daedalus, 100,* 271–304.

Kuhn, T. S. (2000). *The road since structure.* Chicago: University of Chicago Press.

Kuklick, B. (2001). *A history of philosophy in America.* Oxford: Oxford University Press.

Lahr, M. M., & Foley, R. (2004). Human evolution writ small. *Nature, 431,* 1043–1044.

Lakoff, G., & Johnson, M. (1999). *Philosophy in the flesh: The embodied mind and its challenge to Western thought.* New York: Basic Books.

Lamarck, J. B. (1809/1984). *Zoological philosophy* (H. Elliot, Trans.). Chicago: University of Chicago Press.

Lamm, C., Batson, C. D., & Decety, J. (2007). The neural substrate of human empathy: Effects of perspective-taking and cognitive appraisal. *Journal of Cognitive Neuroscience, 19,* 42–58.

Langer, S. (1937). *Philosophy in a new key.* Cambridge, MA: Harvard University Press.

Lashley, K. S. (1951). The problem of serial order in behavior. In L. A. Jeffress (Ed.), *Cerebral mechanisms in behavior.* New York: Wiley and Sons, pp. 112–136.

Latour, B. (1999). *Pandora's hope.* Cambridge, MA: Harvard University Press.

Laudan, L. (1977). *Progress and its problems.* Berkeley: University of California Press.

Lawick-Goodall, J. V. (1971). *In the shadow of man.* London: Collins.

Lawrence, C., & Shapin, S. (Eds.). (1998). *Science incarnate.* Chicago: University of Chicago Press.

Lawson, E. T., & McCauley, R. N. (1990). *Rethinking religion: Connecting cognition and culture.* Cambridge: Cambridge University Press.

Leakey, L. S. B. (1934/1954). *Adam's ancestors.* New York: HarperTorch.

Leakey, R. F., & Lewin, R. (1977). *Origins.* New York: E. P. Dutton.

Le Doux, J. E. (1996). *The emotional brain.* New York: Simon & Schuster.

Lehrman, D. (1958). Induction of broodiness by participation in courtship and nest-building in the ring dove. *Journal of Comparative Physiology and Psychology, 51,* 32–36.

Lennox, J. G. (2001). *Aristotle's philosophy of biology.* Cambridge: Cambridge University Press.

Leslie, A. M. (1987). Pretense and representation: The origins of "theory of mind." *Psychological Review, 94,* 412–426.

Levinson, S. (1996). Language and space. *Annual Review of Anthropology, 25,* 353–382.

Levinson, S. (2003). *Space in language and cognition.* Cambridge: Cambridge University Press.

Levinson, S. (2006). Cognition at the heart of human interaction. *Discourse Studies, 8,* 85–93.

Levinson, S., & Jaisson, P. (Eds.). (2006). *Evolution and culture.* Cambridge, MA: MIT Press.

Lewis, B. (2004). *What went wrong?* Oxford: Oxford University Press.

Lim, M. M., Bielsky, I. F., & Young, L. J. (2005). Neuropeptides and the social brain. *International Journal of Developmental Neuroscience, 23,* 235–243.

Linas, R. R. (2001). *I of the vortex.* Cambridge, MA: MIT Press.

Linnaeus, C. (1735). *Systema naturae.* Leiden: Haak.

Locke, J. (1692–1704/1955). *A letter concerning toleration.* Indianapolis: Bobbs-Merrill.

Loewenstein, G. (1994). The psychology of curiosity. *Psychological Bulletin, 116,* 75–98.

Loewenstein, G. (2006). The pleasures and pains of information. *Science, 312,* 704–706.

Lovejoy, A. O. (1936/1978). *The great chain of being.* Cambridge, MA: Harvard University Press.

Lovejoy, A. O. (1955). *Essays in the history of ideas.* New York: George Braziller.

Lovejoy, C. O. (1978). The origin of man. *Science, 211,* 341–350.

Lowith, K. (1949). *Meaning in history.* Chicago: University of Chicago Press.

Lukas, J. (1968/1997). *Historical consciousness.* New Brunswick, NJ: Transactions.

Lupien, S. J., Maheu, F., Tu, M., Fiocco, A., & Schramek, T. E. (2007). The effects of stress and stress hormones on human cognition: Implications for the field of brain and cognition. *Brain and Cognition, 65,* 209–237.

Lupien, S. J., & McEwen, B. S. (1997). The acute effects of corticosteroids on cognition: Integration of animal and human models studies. *Brain Research, 24,* 1–27.

Lutz, A., Greischar, L. L., Rawling, N. B., Ricard, M., & Davidson, R. J. (2004). Long-term meditators self-induce high-amplitude gamma synchrony during mental practice. *Proceedings of the National Academy of Sciences, 101,* 16369–16373.

Luzatti, F., De Marchis, S., Fasolo, A., & Peretto, P. (2006). Neurogenesis in the caudate nucleus of the adult rabbit. *Journal of Neuroscience, 28,* 609–621.

Lynch, M. P. (1998). *Truth in context.* Cambridge, MA: MIT Press.

Machiavelli, N. (1525/1988). *Florentine histories.* (L. Banfield & H. C. Mansfield, Jr., Trans.). Princeton, NJ: Princeton University Press.

Maess, B., Koelsch, S., Gunter, T. C., & Frederici, A. D. (2001). Musical syntax is processed by Broca's area. *Nature Neuroscience, 4,* 540–545.

Malinowski, B. (1948). *Magic, science and religion.* New York: Doubleday.

Malthus, T. R. (1798/1970). *An essay on the principle of population.* Baltimore: Penguin Books.

Mandler, J. M. (1992). How to build a baby: II, Conceptual primitives. *Psychological Review, 99,* 587–603.

Mandler, J. M. (2004). *The foundations of mind.* Oxford: Oxford University Press.

Margolis, J. (2002). *Reinventing pragmatism: American philosophy at the end of the twentieth century.* Ithaca, NY: Cornell University Press.

Marler, P. (1961). The logical analysis of animal communication. *Journal of Theoretical Biology, 1,* 295–317.

Marler, P. (2000). On innateness. In M. D. Hauser & M. Kinishi (Eds.), *The design of animal communication.* Cambridge, MA: MIT Press, pp. 293–318.

Martin, A., (2007). The representation of object concepts in the brain. *Annual Review of Psychology, 58,* 25–45.

Martin, A., & Caramazza, A. (2003). Neuropsychological and neurimaging perspectives on conceptual knowledge. *Cognitive Neuroscience, 30,* 195–212.

Martin, A., & Weisberg, J. (2003). Neural foundations for understanding social and mechanical concepts. *Cognitive Neuropsychology, 20* (3/4/5/6), 575–587.

Martin, A., Ungerleider, L. G., & Haxby, J. V. (2000). Category specificity and the brain. In M. S. Gazzaniga (Ed.), *The new cognitive neurosciences.* Cambridge, MA: MIT Press, pp. 1023–1036.

Matlock, T. (2004). Fictive motion as cognitive stimulation. *Memory & Cognition, 32,* 1389–1400.

Mayr, E. (1942/1982). *Systemics and the origin of species.* New York: Columbia University Press.

Mayr, E. (1963). *Animal species and evolution.* Cambridge, MA: Harvard University Press.

Mayr, E. (1991). *One long argument.* Cambridge, MA: Harvard University Press.

McCauley, R. N. (2000). The naturalness of religion and the unnaturalness of science. In F. C. Keil & R. A. Wilson (Eds.), *Explanation and cognition.* Cambridge, MA: MIT Press, pp. 61–85.

McCauley, R. N., & Lawson, E. T. (2002). *Bringing ritual to mind.* Cambridge: Cambridge University Press.

McGaugh, J. L. (2000). Memory: A century of consolidation. *Science, 287,* 248–251.

McGaugh, J. L. (2003). *Memory and emotion.* New York: Columbia University Press.

McGinn, C. (1997/1999). *Ethics, evolution and fiction.* Oxford: Oxford University Press.

Mead, G. H. (1934/1972). *Mind, self and society.* Chicago: University of Chicago Press.

Mead, M. (1928). *Coming of age in Samoa.* New York: W. Morrow.

Mead, M. (1964). *Mind in cultural evolution.* New Haven, CT: Yale University Press.

Medin, D. L., & Atran, S. (1999). *Folkbiology.* Cambridge, MA: MIT Press.

Medin, D. L., & Atran, S. (2004). The naïve mind: Biological categorization and reasoning in development and across culture. *Psychological Reviews, 111,* 960–983.

Medvedev, R. (1989). *Let history judge.* New York: Columbia University Press.

Mele, A. R. (2003). *Motivation and agency.* Oxford: Oxford University Press.

Mellars, P. (1996). *Grooming, gossip and the evolution of language.* London: Faber & Faber.

Mellars, P. (2006). Why did modern human populations disperse from Africa ca. 60,000 years ago? *Proceedings of the National Academy of Sciences, 103,* 9381–9386.

Meltzoff, A. N. (2004). The case for developmental cognitive science: Theories of people and things. In G. Bremmer & A. Slater (Eds.), *Theories of infant development.* Oxford, England: Blackwell, pp. 145–173.

Meltzoff, A. N. (2007). "Like me": A foundation for social cognition. *Developmental Science, 10,* 126–134.

Meltzoff, A. N., & Moore, M. K. (1977). Imitation of facial and manual gestures by human neonates. *Science, 198,* 75–78.

Menand, L. (2001). *The metaphysical club.* New York: Farrar, Straus & Giroux.

Merleau-Ponty, M. (1942/1967). *The structure of behavior.* Boston: Beacon Press.

Midgley, M. (1979/1995). *Beast and man.* London: Routledge.

Mill, J. S. (1843/1873). *A system of logic.* London: Longmans, Green, Rader & Dyer.

Ming, G. L., & Song, H. (2005). Adult neurogenesis in the mammalian central nervous system. *Annual Review of Neuroscience, 28,* 223–250.

Mishkin, M., Malamut, B., & Bachevalier, J. (1984). Memories and habits: Two neural systems. In G. Lynch, J. L. McGaugh, & N. M. Weinberger (Eds.), *Neurobiology of learning and memory.* New York: Gulliford, pp. 65–77.

Mishkin, M., Suzuki, W. A., Gadian, D. G., & Vargha-Khadem, F. (1997). Hierarchical organization of cognitive memory. *Philosophical Transactions of the Royal Society of London, 352,* 1461–1467.

Mistlberger, R. E. (1994). Circadian food anticipatory activity: Formal models and physiological mechanisms. *Neuroscience & Biobehavioral Reviews, 18,* 171–195.

Mithen, S. (1996). *The prehistory of the mind: The cognitive origins of art and science.* London: Thames & Hudson.

Mithen, S. (2006). *The singing Neanderthal.* Cambridge, MA: Harvard University Press.

Modahl, C., Green, L., Fein, D., Morris, M., Waterhouse, L., Feinstein, C., et al. (1998). Plasma oxytocin levels in autistic children. *Biological Psychiatry, 43,* 270–277.

Moll, J., de Oliveira-Souza, R., & Eslinger, P. J. (2003). Morals and the human brain: A working model. *NeuroReport, 14,* 299–305.

Moore, J. A. (1993). *Science as a way of knowing.* Cambridge, MA: Harvard University Press.

Moore-Ede, M. C., Sulzman, F. M., & Fuller, C. A. (1992). *The clocks that time us.* Cambridge, MA: Harvard University Press.

Moreno, J. D. (2003). Neuroethics: An agenda for neuroscience and society. *Nature Reviews Neuroscience, 4,* 149–153.

Muir, J. (1912/1962). *The Yosemite.* New York: Doubleday.

Muramoto, O. (2004). The role of the medial prefrontal cortex in human religious activity. *Medical Hypotheses, 62,* 479–485.

Murphy, G. L. (2002). *The big book of concepts.* Cambridge, MA: MIT Press.

Nash, R. (1967). *Wilderness and the American mind.* New Haven, CT: Yale University Press.

Nelissen, K., Luppino, G., Vanduffel, W., Rizzolatti, G., & Orban, G. A. (2005). Observing others: Multiple action representation in the frontal lobe. *Science, 310,* 332–336.

Nelson, R. J. (1995). *An introduction to behavioral endocrinology.* Sunderland, MA: Sinauer Associates.

Neville, R. C. (1974). *The cosmology of freedom.* New Haven, CT: Yale University Press.

Neville, R. C. (1992). *Highroad around modernism.* Albany: State University of New York Press.

Nichols, N., & Stitch, S. P. (2003). *Mindreading.* Oxford: Oxford University Press.

Nunes, C. R., Pelz, K. M., Muecke, E. M., Holekamp, K. E., & Zucker, I. (2006). Plasma glucocorticoid concentrations and body mass in ground squirrels: Seasonal variation and circannual organization. *General and Comparative Endocrinology, 146*, 136–163.

Nussbaum, M. C. (1997). *Cultivating humanity.* Cambridge, MA: Harvard University Press.

Nussbaum, M. C. (2004). *Hiding from humanity.* Princeton, NJ: Princeton University Press.

Nye, M. J. (1996). *Before big science.* Cambridge, MA: Harvard University Press.

Oakes, G. (1988). *Weber and Rickert.* Cambridge, MA: MIT Press.

Oelschlaeger, M. (1991). *The idea of wilderness.* New Haven, CT: Yale University Press.

Okamoto-Barth, S., Call, J., & Tomasello, M. (2007). Great apes' understanding of other individuals' line of sight. *Psychological Science, 18*, 462–468.

Opfer, J. E., & Gelman, S. A. (2001). Children's and adult's models for predicting teleological action: The development of a biology-based model. *Child Development, 72*, 1367–1381.

Otto, R. (1923/1975). *The idea of the holy.* Oxford: Oxford University Press.

Paabo, S. (2001). The human genome and our view of ourselves. *Science, 291*, 1219–1220.

Panksepp, J. (1998). *Affective neuroscience: The foundations of human and animal emotions.* New York: Oxford University.

Parrott, W. G., & Schulkin, J. (1993). Neuropsychology and the cognitive nature of the emotions. *Cognition and Emotion, 7*, 43–59.

Paton, J. A., & Nottebohm, F. N. (1984). Neurons generated in the adult brain are recruited into functional circuits. *Science, 225*, 1046–1048.

Pauly, P. J. (1987). *Controlling life.* Oxford: Oxford University Press.

Paus, T. (2001). Primate anterior cingulate cortex: Where motor control, drive and cognition interface. *Nature Reviews Neuroscience, 2*, 417–424.

Peirce, C. S. (1878). Deduction, induction and hypothesis. *Popular Science Monthly, 13*, 470–82.

Peirce, C. S. (1892). The architecture of theories. *The Monist, 1*, 61–76.

Peirce, C. S. (1893/1992). Evolutionary love. In N. Houser & C. Kloesel (Eds.), *The essential Peirce: Vol. 1.* Bloomington: Indiana University Press, pp. 352–362.

Peirce, C. S. (1893/1936). *Religion and science: Collected works* (E. Hartshorne & P. Weiss, Eds.). Cambridge, MA: Harvard University Press.

Peirce, C. S. (1899/1992). *Reasoning and the logic of things* (K. L. Ketner & H. Putnam, Eds.). Cambridge, MA: Harvard University Press.

Peirce, C. S. (1908/1998). A neglected argument for the reality of god. In N. Houser et al. (Eds.), *The essential Peirce: Vol. 2*. Bloomington: Indiana University Press, pp. 434–451.

Perani, D., Cappa, S. F., Bettinardi, V., Bressi, S., Gorno-Tempini, M., Matarrese, M., et al. (1995). Different neural systems for the recognition of animals and man-made tools. *Neuroreport, 6*, 1636–1641.

Perrett, D., Harries, M., Bevan, R., Thomas, S., Benson, P., Mistlin, A., et al. (1989). Frameworks of analysis for the neural representation of animate objects and actions. *Journal of Experimental Biology, 146*, 87–113.

Piaget, J. (1954). *The construction of reality in the child*. New York: Basic Books.

Piaget, J. (1971/1975). *Biology and knowledge*. Chicago: University of Chicago Press.

Pinker, S. (1994). *The language instinct*. New York: William Morrow.

Pinker, S. (1997). *How the mind works*. New York: W. W. Norton.

Pinker, S. (2007). *The stuff of thought*. New York: Viking.

Plato (1941). *The republic*. Oxford: Oxford University Press.

Plotkin, H. (1993). *Darwin machines*. Cambridge, MA: Harvard University Press.

Polanyi, M. (1946/1964). *Science, faith and society*. Chicago: University of Chicago Press.

Premack, D. (1990). The infant's theory of self-propelled objects. *Cognition, 36*, 1–16.

Premack, D., & Premack, A. J. (1983). *The mind of the ape*. New York: W. W. Norton.

Prinz, J. J. (2004). *Gut reactions*. Oxford: Oxford University Press.

Prinz, J. J., & Barsalou, L. W. (2000). Steering a course for embodied representation. In E. Dietrich & A. B. Markman (Eds.), *Cognitive dynamics: Conceptual change in humans and machines*. Mahwah, NJ: Lawrence Erlbaum, pp. 51–77.

Pulvermuller, F., Shtyrov, Y., & Ilmoniemi, R. (2005). Brain signatures of meaning in action word recognition. *Journal of Cognitive Neuroscience, 6*, 884–892.

Putnam, H. (1990). *Realism with a human face*. Cambridge, MA: Harvard University Press.

Quine, W. V. O. (1953/1961). *From a logical point of view*. New York: HarperTorch.

Quine, W. V. O. (1969). Epistemology naturalized. In *Ontological relativity and other essays*. New York: Columbia University Press, pp. 69–90.

Rakison, D. H., & Dubois, D. P. (2001). Developmental origins of the animate-inanimate distinction. *Psychological Bulletin, 127*, 209–228.

Rakison, D. H., & Oakes, L. M. (2003). *Early category and concept develop-ment.* Oxford: Oxford University Press.

Reschler, N. (2000). *Nature and understanding.* Oxford, England: Clarendon Press.

Rescorla, R. A., & Wagner, A. R. (1972). A theory of Pavlovian conditioning; Variations in the effectiveness of reinforcement and nonreinforcement. In A. H. Black & W. F. Prokasy, (Eds.), *Classical conditioning.* New York: Appleton-Century-Crofts, pp. 64–99.

Richards, R. J. (1992/1995). *The meaning of evolution.* Chicago: University of Chicago Press.

Richter, C. P. (1943). *Total self-regulatory functions in animals and man.* New York: Harvey Lecture Series.

Richter, C. P. (1965/1979). *Biological clocks in medicine and psychiatry.* Spring-field, IL: Charles C. Thomas.

Rickert, H. (1929/1986). *The limits of concept formation in natural science* (G. Oakes, Trans.). Cambridge: Cambridge University Press.

Rizzolatti, G., & Luppino, G. (2001). The cortical motor system. *Neuron, 31,* 889–901.

Rohrer, T. (2001). Pragmatism, ideology and embodiment: William James and the philosophical foundations of cognitive linguistics. In *Language and ideology: Cognitive theoretical approaches.* Amsterdam: John Benjamins, pp. 49–81.

Rolls, E. T., & Treves, A. (1998). *Neural networks and brain function.* New York: Oxford University Press.

Romer, A. S. (1968). *Vertebrate paleontology.* Chicago: University of Chicago Press.

Roozendaal, B. (2000). Glucocorticoids and the regulation of memory con-solidation. *Psychoneuroendocrinology, 25,* 213–238.

Rorty, R. (1999). *Philosophy and social hope.* New York: Penguin Books.

Rose, S. (1998). *Lifelines.* Oxford: Oxford University Press.

Rosen, J. B., & Schulkin, J. (1998). From normal fear to pathological anxiety. *Psychological Review, 105,* 325–350.

Rosenberg, A. (2006). *Darwinian reductionism.* Chicago: University of Chicago Press.

Rosenwasser, A. M. (2003). Neurobiology of the mammalian circadian sys-tem: Oscillators, pacemakers and pathways. In S. J. Fluharty & H. J. Grill (Eds.), *Progress in psychobiology and physiological psychology,* Vol. 18. New York: Elsevier, pp. 1–38.

Rosenwasser, A. M., Schulkin, J., & Adler, N. T. (1988). Anticipatory appeti-tive behavior of adrenalectomized rats under circadian salt-access sched-ules. *Animal Learning and Behavior, 16,* 324–329.

Rosenzweig, M. R. (1984). Experience, memory and the brain. *American Psychology, 39*, 365–376.

Royce, J. (1912/1940). *The sources of religious insight.* New York: Charles Scribner's Sons.

Rozin, P. (1976). The evolution of intelligence and access to the cognitive unconscious. In J. Sprague & A. N. Epstein (Eds.), *Progress in psychobiology and physiological psychology.* New York: Academic Press, pp. 245–280.

Rozin, P. (1998). Evolution and development of brains and cultures. In M. S. Gazzaniga & J. S. Altman (Eds.), *Brain and mind: Evolutionary perspectives.* France: Human Frontiers Sciences Program, pp. 111–125.

Rozin, P. (2005). The meaning of natural: Process more important than content. *Psychological Science, 16*, 652–658.

Rozin, P., & Fallon, A. E. (1987). A perspective on disgust. *Psychological Review, 94*, 23–41.

Rozin, P., & Schulkin, J. (1990). Food selection. In E. M. Stricker (Ed.), *Handbook of behavioral biology, Volume 10: Food and fluid intake.* New York: Plenum Press, pp. 297–328.

Rubin, D. C. (2005). A basic-systems approach to autobiographical memory. *Current Directions in Psychological Science, 14*, 79–83.

Ruby, N. F., Dark, J., Burns, D. E., Heller, H. C., & Zucker, I. (2002). The suprachiasmatic nucleus is essential for circadian body temperature rhythms in hibernating ground squirrels. *Journal of Neuroscience, 22*, 357–364.

Ruby, P., & Decety, J. (2001). Effects of subjective perspective during simulation of action: A PET investigation of agency. *Nature Neuroscience, 4*, 546–550.

Rue, L. (2005). *Religion is not about God.* New Brunswick, NJ: Rutgers University Press.

Runciman, W. G., Smith, J. M., & Dunbar, R. I. M. (Eds.). (1996). *Evolution of social behaviour patterns in primates and man.* New York: Oxford University Press.

Rusak, B., & Zucker, I. (1979). Neural regulation of circadian rhythms. *Physiological Review, 59*, 499–526.

Ruse, M. (2006). *Darwinism and its discontents.* Cambridge: Cambridge University Press.

Russell, R. J., Murphy, N., Meyering, T. C., & Arbib, M. A. (2002). *Neuroscience and the person.* Rome: Vatican Observatory Foundation.

Ryle, G. (1949). *The concept of mind.* London: Hutchinson.

Sabini, J., & Schulkin, J. (1994). Biological realism and social constructivism. *Journal for the Theory of Social Behavior, 224*, 207–217.

Sabini, J., & Silver, M. (1982). *Moralities of everyday life.* Oxford: Oxford University Press.

Sagoff, M. (1988). *The economy of the earth.* Cambridge: Cambridge University Press.

Santayana, G. (1932/1967). *Character and opinion in the United States.* New York: W. W. Norton.

Sapolsky, R. M. (1992). *Stress: The aging brain and the mechanisms of neuron death.* Cambridge, MA: MIT Press.

Sarokin, D., & Schulkin, J. (1994). Co-evolution of rights and environmental justice. *The Environmentalist, 14,* 121–129.

Savan, D. (1981). Peirce's semiotic theory of emotion. In K. L. Ketner et al. (Eds.), *Proceedings of the Charles S. Peirce Bicentennial International Congress.* Lubbock: Texas Tech Press, pp. 319–333.

Saver, J. L., & Rabin, J. (1997). The neural substrates of religious experience. *Journal of Neuropsychiatry, 9,* 498–510.

Saxe, R., Tzelnic, T., & Carey, S. (2006). Five-month-old infants know humans are solid, like inanimate objects. *Cognition, 101,* B1–B8.

Schacter, D. L. (1996). *Searching for memory.* New York: Basic Books.

Schacter, D. L., & Addis, D. R. (2007). The cognitive neuroscience of constructive memory: Remembering the past and imagining the future. *Philosophical Transactions of the Royal Society, 362,* 773–786.

Schacter, D. L., & Tulving, E. (1994). *Memory systems.* Cambridge, MA: MIT Press.

Schama, S. (1995). *Landscapes and memory.* New York: Vintage Books.

Schelling, F. W. J. (1797/1988). *Ideas for a philosophy of nature* (E. E. Harris & P. Heath, Eds.). Cambridge: Cambridge University Press.

Scheler, M. (1928/1976). *Man's place in nature* (H. Meyerhoff, Trans.). New York: Noonday Press.

Schliermacher, F. (1799/1958). *On religion.* New York: Harper & Row.

Schmidt, L. A., & Schulkin, J. (Eds.). (1999). *Extreme fear, shyness, and social phobia: Origins, biological mechanisms, and clinical outcome.* (Series in Affective Science). New York: Oxford University Press.

Schneider, H. W. (1946/1963). *A history of American philosophy.* New York: Columbia University Press.

Schulkin, J. (1991). *Sodium hunger.* Cambridge: Cambridge University Press.

Schulkin, J. (1992). *The pursuit of inquiry.* Albany: State University of New York Press.

Schulkin, J. (1996). *The delicate balance.* Lanham, MD: University Press of America.

Schulkin, J. (1999). *The neuroendocrine regulation of behavior.* Cambridge: Cambridge University Press.

Schulkin, J. (2000). *Roots of social sensibility and neural function.* Cambridge, MA: MIT Press.

Schulkin, J. (2003). *Rethinking homeostasis.* Cambridge, MA: MIT Press.

Schulkin, J. (2004). *Bodily sensibility: Intelligent action.* Oxford: Oxford University Press.

Schulkin, J., (2005). *Curt Richter: A life in the laboratory.* Baltimore: Johns Hopkins University Press.

Schulkin, J. (2007a). *Effort: A neurobiological perspective on the will.* New York: Lawrence Erlbaum Associates.

Schulkin, J. (2007b). Autism and the amygdala: An endocrine hypothesis. *Brain and Cognition, 65,* 87–99.

Schultz, W. (2002). Getting formal with dopamine and reward. *Neuron, 36,* 241–263.

Schultz, W. (2004). Neural coding of basic reward terms of animal learning, game theory, microeconomics and behavioral ecology. *Current Opinion in Neurobiology, 14,* 139–147.

Schumpeter, J. A. (1934). *Theory of economic development.* Cambridge, MA: Harvard University Press.

Schutz, A. (1932/1967). *The phenomenology of the social world* (G. Walsh & F. Lehnert, Eds.). Chicago: Northwestern University Press.

Sellars, W. (1962). *Science, perception, and reality.* New York: Routledge & Kegan.

Sellars, W. (1968). *Science and metaphysics.* New York: Humanities Press.

Seneca (1969). *Letters from a stoic.* New York: Penguin Classics.

Shade, P. (2001). *Habits of hope: A pragmatic theory.* Nashville, TN: Vanderbilt University Press.

Shapin, S. (1995). *A social history of truth.* Chicago: University of Chicago Press.

Shapin, S. (1996). *The scientific revolution.* Chicago: University of Chicago Press.

Shapiro, L. A. (2004). *The mind incarnate.* Cambridge, MA: MIT Press.

Shelley, M. (1817/1976). *Frankenstein.* New York: Pyram.

Shook, J. R. (Ed.). (2003). *Pragmatic naturalism and realism.* Amherst, NY: Prometheus Press.

Shors, T. J., Micseages, C., Beylin, A., Zhao, M., Rydel, T., & Gould, E. (2001). Neurogenesis in the adult is involved in the formation of trace memories. *Nature, 410,* 372–375.

Simon, H. A. (1962). The architecture of complexity. *Proceedings of the American Philosophical Society, 106,* 470–473.

Simon, H. A. (1982). *Models of bounded rationality.* Cambridge, MA: MIT Press.

Simon, H. A. (1990). Invariants of human behavior. *Annual Review of Psychology, 41*, 1–20.

Simpson, G. (1961). *Principles of animal taxonomy.* New York: Columbia University Press.

Simpson, G. G. (1949). *The meaning of evolution.* New Haven, CT: Yale University Press.

Simpson, G. G. (1980). *Splendid isolation.* New Haven, CT: Yale University Press.

Skrbina, D. (2005). *Panpsychism in the West.* Cambridge, MA: MIT Press.

Smith, J. E. (1970). *Themes in American philosophy.* New York: Harper-Torch/Harper & Row.

Smith, J. E. (1978). *Purpose and thought.* New Haven, CT: Yale University Press.

Smith, J. E. (1985). Experience in Peirce, James and Dewey. *Monist, 68*, 538–554.

Smith, L., & Gasser, M. (2005). The development of embodied cognition: Six lessons from babies. *Artificial Life, 11*, 13–29.

Smith, W. J. (1977). *The behavior of communicating: An ethological approach.* Cambridge, MA: Harvard University Press.

Snow, C. P. (1961). *Science and government.* Cambridge, MA: Harvard University Press.

Solomon, R. C. (2002). *Spirituality for the skeptic.* Oxford: Oxford University Press.

Spelke, E. S., Phillips, A., & Woodward, A. L. (1995). Infants' knowledge of object motion and human action. In D. Sperber, D. Premack, & A. J. Premack (Eds.), *Causal cognition: A multidisciplinary debate.* Oxford, England: Clarendon Press, pp. 44–77.

Sperber, D. (1975). *Rethinking symbolism.* Cambridge: Cambridge University Press.

Sperber, D. (1985). *On anthropological knowledge.* Cambridge: Cambridge University Press.

Spezio, M. L., Adolphs, R., Hurley, R. S., & Piven, J. (2007). Analysis of face gaze in autism using "bubbles." *Neuropsychologia, 45*, 144–151.

Spinoza, B. (1668/1955). *On the improvement of the understanding* (R. H. M. Elwes, Ed.). New York: Dover Press.

Squire, L. R. (1987). *Memory and brain.* New York: Oxford University Press.

Squire, L. R. (2004). Memory systems of the brain: A brief history and current perspective. *Neurobiology of Learning and Memory, 82*, 171–177.

Squire, L. R., & Zola, S. M. (1998). Episodic memory, semantic memory, and amnesia. *Hippocampus, 8*, 205–211.

Sterelny, K. (2000). *The evolution of agency and other essays.* Cambridge: Cambridge University Press.

Sterelny, K. (2003). *Thought in a hostile world.* New York: Blackwell.

Sterelny, K. (2004). Genes, memes and human history. *Mind and Language, 19,* 249–57.

Sterling, P. (2004). Principles of allostasis. In J. Schulkin (Ed.), *Allostasis, homeostasis and the costs of physiological adaptation.* Cambridge: Cambridge University Press, pp. 17–64.

Sterling, P., & Eyer, J. (1988). Allostasis: A new paradigm to explain arousal pathology. In S. Fisher & J. Reason (Eds.), *Handbook of life stress: Cognition and health.* New York: John Wiley & Sons, pp. 629–648.

Suddendorf, T., & Corballis, M. C. (1997). Mental time travel and the evolution of the human mind. *Genetic Social and General Psychology Monographs, 123,* 133–167.

Suddendorf, T., & Corballis, M. C. (2007). The evolution of foresight. *Behavioral and Brain Sciences, 30,* 299–313.

Swanson, L. W. (2000). Cerebral hemisphere regulation of motivated behavior. *Brain Research, 886,* 113–164.

Swanson, L. W. (2003). *Brain architecture.* Oxford: Oxford University Press.

Tattersall, I. (1993). *The human odyssey: Four million years of human evolution.* New York: Prentice Hall.

Taupin, P., & Gage, F. H. (2002). Adult neurogenesis and neural stem cell of the central nervous system. *Journal of Neuroscience Research, 69,* 745–749.

Taylor, C. (2002). *Varieties of religion today.* Cambridge, MA: Harvard University Press.

Taylor, C. (2007). *A secular age.* Cambridge, MA: Harvard University Press.

Thomas, E. (2001). Empathy and consciousness. *Journal of Consciousness Studies, 8,* 1–35.

Thoreau, H. D. (1971). *Great short works.* New York: Harper & Row.

Thucydides (1989). *The Peloponnesian wars* (T. Hobbes, Trans.). Chicago: University of Chicago Press.

Tillich, P. (1951/1967). *Systematic theology* (Vols. 1–2). Chicago: University of Chicago Press.

Todes, D. P. (1989). *Darwin without Malthus.* Oxford: Oxford University Press.

Todes, D. P. (1997). Pavlov's physiology factory. *History of Science Society, 88,* 205–46.

Tolman, E. C. (1949). *Purposive behavior in animals and men.* Berkeley: University of California Press.

Tomasello, M., & Call, J. (1997). *Primate cognition.* Oxford: Oxford University Press.

Tomasello, M., & Carpenter, M. (2007). Shared intentionality. *Developmental Science, 10,* 121–125.

Tomasello, M., Carpenter, M., Call, J., Behne, T., & Moll, H. (2004). Understanding and sharing intentions: The origins of cultural cognition. *Behavioral and Brain Sciences, 28,* 675–735.

Tomasello, M., Savage-Rumbaugh, E. S., & Kruger, A. C. (1993). Imitative learning of actions on objects by children, chimpanzees, and enculturated chimpanzees. *Child Development, 64,* 688–705.

Tooby, J., & Cosmides, L. (1992). The psychological foundations of culture. In J. H. Barkow, L. Cosmides, & J. Tooby (Eds.), *The adaptive mind.* New York: Oxford University Press, pp. 19–136.

Toulmin, S. (1977). *Human understanding.* Princeton, NJ: Princeton University Press.

Toulmin, S. (2001). *Return to reason.* Cambridge, MA: Harvard University Press.

Tulving, E. (1983/1993). *Elements of episodic memory.* Oxford, England: Clarendon Press.

Tulving, E. (2002). Episodic memory: From mind to brain. *Annual Review of Psychology, 53,* 1–25.

Tulving, E., & Craik, F. I. M. (2000). *The Oxford handbook of memory.* Oxford: Oxford University Press.

Tzu, C. (1962). *The writing of Chuang Tzu.* New York: Dover Press.

Ullman, M. T. (2001). A neurocognitive perspective on language: The declarative procedural model. *Nature Neuroscience, 9,* 266–286.

Ullman, M. T. (2004). Is Broca's area part of a basal ganglia thalamocortical circuit? *Cognition, 92,* 231–270.

Van Prang, H., Christie, B. R., Sejnowski, T. J., & Gage, F. H. (1999). Running enhances neurogenesis, learning and long-term potentiation in mice. *Proceedings of the National Academy of Sciences, 96,* 13427–13431.

Varela, F. J., Thompson, E., & Rosch, E. (1991). *The embodied mind.* Cognitive Science and Human Experience Series. Cambridge, MA: MIT Press.

Vico, G. (1744/1970). *The new sciences.* Ithaca, NY: Cornell University Press.

Wang, A. T., Dapretto, M., Hariri, A. R., Sigman, M., & Bookheimer, S. Y. (2004). Neural correlates of facial affect processing in children and adolescents with autism spectrum disorder. *Journal of the American Academy of Child and Adolescent Psychiatry, 43,* 481–490.

Warrington, E. K., & Shallice, T. (1984). Category-specific semantic impairment. *Brain, 107,* 829–854.

Waxman, S. R. (1999). The dubbing ceremony revisited: Object naming and categorization in infancy and early childhood. In D. L. Medin & S. Atran (Eds.), *Folkbiology*. Cambridge, MA: MIT Press, pp. 232–284.

Waxman, S. R. (2007). Folkbiological reasoning from a cross-cultural developmental perspective: Early essentialist notions are shaped by cultural beliefs. *Developmental Psychology, 43,* 294–308.

Weber, M. (1905/1958). *The Protestant ethic and the spirit of capitalism* (T. Parkson, Trans.). New York: Scribner's.

Weber, M. (1947). *The theory of social and economic organization* (A. Henderston & T. Parsons, Trans.). New York: Free Press.

Wehr, T. A., Moul, D. E., Barbato, G., Giesen, H. A., Seidel, J. A., Barker, C., et al. (1993). Conservation of photoperiod-responsive mechanisms in humans. *American Journal of Physiology, 265,* 846–857.

Weidman, N. M. (1999). *Constructing scientific psychology.* Cambridge: Cambridge University Press.

Weisberg, J., Turennout, M., & Martin, A. (2006). A neural system for learning about object function. *Cerebral Cortex, 17,* 513–521.

Wells, G. (1999). *Dialogic inquiry.* Cambridge: Cambridge University Press.

Wellman, H. (1990). *The child's theory of mind.* Cambridge, MA: MIT Press.

Weissman, D. (2000). *A social ontology.* New Haven, CT: Yale University Press.

Weissman, D. (2008). *Styles of thought.* Albany: State University of New York Press.

Wells, G. (1999). *Dialogic inquiry: Toward a sociocultural practice and theory of education.* Cambridge: Cambridge University Press.

Wheatley, T., Milleville, S. C., & Martin, A. (2007). Understanding animate agents. *Psychological Science, 18,* 469–474.

Wheeler, M. (2005). *Reconstructing the cognitive world.* Cambridge, MA: MIT Press.

Whitehead, A. N. (1927/1953). *Symbolism.* New York: Macmillan.

Whitehead, A. N. (1929/1957). *The aims of education.* New York: Free Press.

Whitehead, A. N. (1929/1958). *The function of reason.* Boston: Beacon Press.

Whitehead, A. N. (1933/1961). *Adventures of ideas.* New York: Free Press.

Whitehead, A. N. (1938/1967). *Modes of thought.* New York: Free Press.

Whiten, A., & Byrne, R. W. (Eds.). (1997). *Machiavellian intelligence II: Extensions and evaluations.* Cambridge: Cambridge University Press.

Williams, W. C. (1949/1969). *Selected poems.* New York: New Directions Press.

Wilson, E. O. (1994). *Naturalist.* Washington, DC: Island Press.

Wilson, E. O. (1995). *Consilience: The unity of knowledge.* New York: Alfred A. Knopf.

Wilson, M. (2002). Six views of embodied cognition. *Psychonomic Bulletin and Review, 9*, 625–636.

Wilson, M., & Knoblich, G. (2005). The case for motor involvement in perceiving conspecifics. *Psychological Bulletin, 131*, 460–473.

Wilson, R. A. (Ed.). (1999). *Species: New interdisciplinary essays.* Cambridge, MA: MIT Press.

Wilson, R. A. (2004). *Boundaries of the mind.* Cambridge: Cambridge University Press.

Wilson, R. A. (2005). *Genes and the agents of life.* Cambridge: Cambridge University Press.

Wingfield, J. C. (2004). Allostatic load and life cycles: Implication for neuroendocrine control mechanisms. In J. Schulkin (Ed.), *Allostasis, homeostasis and the costs of physiological adaptation.* Cambridge: Cambridge University Press, pp. 302–342.

Wittgenstein, L. (1953/1968). *Philosophical investigations.* New York: Macmillan.

Wolff, P., & Medin, D. L. (2001). Measuring the evolution and devolution of folk-biological knowledge. In L. Maffi (Ed.), *On biocultural diversity: Linking language, knowledge, and the environment.* Washington, DC: Smithsonian Institution, pp. 212–227.

Woodward, C. V. (1955/1966). *The strange career of Jim Crow.* New York: Oxford University Press.

Woodward, C. V. (1986). *Thinking back.* Baton Rouge: Louisiana State University.

Woodward, C. V. (1989). *Future of the past.* Oxford: Oxford University Press.

Worster, D. (1977/1991). *Nature's economy.* Cambridge: Cambridge University Press.

Wu, S., Jia, M., Ruan, Y., Liu, J., Guo, Y., Shuang, M., et al. (2005). Positive association of the oxytocin receptor gene (OXTR) with autism in the Chinese Han population. *Biological Psychiatry, 58*, 74–77.

Wuerfel, J., Krischamoorthy, E. S., Brown, R. J., Lemieus, L., Koepp, M., Tebartz van Elst, L., et al. (2004). Religiosity is associated with hippocampal, but not amygdala volume in patients with refractory epilepsy. *Journal of Neurology, Neurosurgery and Psychiatry, 75*, 640–642.

Young, A. W. (1998). *Face and mind.* Oxford: Oxford University Press.

Zeki, S. (1999). Art and the brain. *Journal of Consciousness Studies, 6*, 76–96.

Zucker, I. (1988). Neuroendocrine substrates of circannual rhythms. In D. J. Kufpler, T. R. Monk, & J. D. Barchas (Eds.), *Biological rhythms and mental disorders.* New York: Guilford Press, pp. 219–251.

INDEX